State of the Economy

The Failure of Healthcare in the U.S.

By: Andrew Shecktor

State of the Economy

The Failure of Healthcare in the U.S.

Copyright © 2016 Shecktor Enterprises, Inc.

ISBN-13: 978-1546966180

ISBN-10: 1546966188

Printed in USA by CreateSpace

Dedication

This publication is dedicated to all the hard workers in our U.S. Government offices who have dedicated so much time to collecting and compiling data on our country and our economy, and to all the great people that have put together the many charts and graphs contained herein.

I also wish to thank all the poor souls who have had to listen to me rant and rave, and who have made suggestions which helped move this project forward. I have graciously accepted the good, the bad and the ugly. During the course of my research I have spoken with people of all political persuasions and of all race, creed and gender, and have become a more enlightened person because of this. I will never be able to thank all these people who took time out of their lives to sit and speak with me – even when our opinions differed.

So, simply put, thank you everyone who participated in this ongoing quest for knowledge. I am certain there will be more to come!

***

We have a crisis in the United States today. Our economy is failing, and few people even realize it. The loss of jobs to automation and the loss of our workforce due to public assistance and disability are crippling our country. Statistically, only 62 percent the U.S. workforce is employed (and 13 percent is underemployed), compared to over 90 percent in the U.K. and other civilized nations. People are shocked at the middle class revolution and the emergence of Donald Trump as president, yet no one seems to understand the real cause of the disease and distress of our nation. The hope of this document is to bring to light the causes of our perilous downhill trend. It is backed by graphs, charts and references from verified government and official sources. It is now up to us to decide, will we continue down the path of becoming a welfare state, or will we get off the couch and get back to work.

Table of Contents

About the Author

Andrew Shecktor was born in 1956 and grew up in the small Philadelphia suburb of Plymouth Meeting. He has published numerous articles and fiction, including the novella "Centralia PA, Devils Fire," a fictional encounter with the town of Centralia PA, which was vacated due to an ongoing underground mine fire.

He has been involved in Republican politics since 1970 and has been involved in every election since then.

In his early years he was a member of the Teenage Republicans and of the Jaycees. He worked for U.S. Congressman Laurence Coughlin (deceased, 13th PA Congressional district) and while in his employ assisted in the penning of several pieces of legislation.

Mr. Shecktor was a member of the Congressional Computer Advisory Committee under U.S. Congressman Jon Fox (13th PA Congressional District.)

He was instrumental in many elections over the years, but only recently became personally involved in politics. He ran for Mayor of Berwick, PA in 2013. He lost, but received 42 percent of the vote against the most popular person in the borough. He was appointed to the Berwick Planning Commission in 2015 and ran for Council that year. He won the election and a 4 year seat on the council where he was appointed to law and finance and emergency management committees.

In 2016 he ran for delegate to the Republican National Convention. After an epic campaign, meeting over 25,000 people, attending events and making radio and TV appearances he handily won the election, despite placing second to last in a field of 15 and appearing on page 2 of the ballot (you had to actually find page two to find his name.)

As of this writing he is running for a long shot in the 2018 Pennsylvania U.S. Senatorial elections to unseat incumbent Bob Casey.

Mr. Shecktor is a 40 year veteran of the fire service and works with many other emergency services and volunteer community services. He is also a ham radio operator and has worked as a paralegal in the past.

Preface

This presentation is the culmination of over 2 years of research and 6 months of more or less daily updates and tweaking.

It is based on verifiable facts from trusted sources, all of which have been verified and cross referenced. All sources are listed in this document.

The author has attempted to present a non-partisan, unbiased interpretation of the current state of the economy in the United States, and what is needed to resolve our current situation, which is far worse than the media or politicians would have us believe.

The proxy used in this presentation is the healthcare situation, though the statistics are relevant to all aspects of the American economy, and indeed across the world. The author also has a particular interest in healthcare, as he has been a victim of the ACA (which he refuses to spell out since it is anything but affordable to most.) Not only has his insurance out of pocket gone from $500.00 to $5,000.00 overnight, but his wife was dropped to part time (less than 30 hours per week) and lost her insurance. Now the cost of her insurance exceeds her monthly take home pay! This was the start of the author's path to find out where the healthcare plan failed us, and why some people are so enthralled by it.

As it turns out, those with extremely low income and those with preexisting conditions stand behind the ACA. Of course they do. They have the single payer, universal health insurance that everyone yearns for. Those on public assistance full time also have the "basic income" that some countries are beginning to consider.

The problem, it turns out, is that someone has to pay for all this. Those paying are the middle class, particularly the lower middle class, who can no longer afford their own health care because they are paying for those who are not working. As this project progressed it became obvious that the root cause of our healthcare failure, the love/hate relationship with the Obama ACA and even the "Trump Phenomenon" are all the outcome of a failed economy that has divided the city dweller from the country dweller, the wealthy from the poor, and which has left the rural middle class stranded high and dry.

In times past, the free market system worked for everything, including healthcare. The question now is – has the capitalist system become too greedy and corrupt to be trusted to regulate themselves, or is just that no one is working to pay for services and thus defray their cost.

The author is not attempting to promote any personal agenda, but is of the firm belief that no human being in our country, regardless of their ability to pay, should go without adequate healthcare, including routine checkups, emergency care and follow ups. No human should be treated specially or differently regarding healthcare. No person should fear going to a doctor or hospital for needed medical care in fear of not being able to pay, or any other reason. No one should die because they couldn't pay for needed medical services. Does this mean single payer, universal life, or could the old free market system work? That is for you to decide, but either way, the system needs people working to pay for it. In the United States more people are out of work today than were out of work at the height of the Great Depression in 1932. We have been sold a bill of goods on our economy. Our businesses are doing great thanks to computers and automation; our citizens not so much.

Chapter One

Our economic failure

This project began when a question that was asked regarding healthcare in the United States. Why is it that we ended up with such a poorly conceived heath plan (the not so affordable "Affordable Healthcare Act"), and what created the immovable rift between those insist we should have free market healthcare and those who insist we need universal, single payer healthcare. Health care will be the primary example in this document, but the information is equally relevant to all products and services.

As a conservative I always believed that the market for services should be self-regulating with no government interference. It worked just fine through the 1980's or so. Prices for healthcare were cheap, copays and deductibles were low. Then the bottom fell out. Prices began to climb and out of pocket costs went up.

In 1993, during the Presidency of Bill Clinton, Hillary Clinton proposed a government run healthcare plan as more and more poor and low paid workers were unable to purchase health insurance. The proposal did not pass and it was lost to history.

When Barack Obama took office in 2008 the idea of government funded healthcare was rekindled, and passed as the "The Patient Protection and Affordable Care Act" shortened to "The Affordable Care Act." It became known to those opposing it as "Obamacare," a derogatory nickname insinuating that the plan is totally worthless and beyond redemption. Supporters quote the millions who had no insurance, but now have it. They fail, however, to report the millions of middle class workers who LOST their insurance, and in many cases many hours of work, due to the clause that states that businesses don't need to provide insurance to part time employees (working under 30 hours.) The assumption here is that those workers will buy insurance on the Marketplace and get subsidies from the government to help pay the premiums (these subsidies are stripped from the middle class paycheck, causing the middle class to pay unaffordable.) They also don't tell you of the phenomenally ridiculous copays, deductibles and other out of pocket costs levied on all but the poorest recipients of Medicaid or Marketplace insurance. Obama "Tell" robbed from the "rich" to give to the poor! Finally, they base the affordability of healthcare on the family unit. Thus, if there is one person in a family supporting the household and another goes to work part time or at a low paying job, the cost of the mandatory health care or the penalty cost for not having insurance may actually EXCEED the take home pay of the worker!

The healthcare issue is one of the primary reasons that the middle class rose up and revolted and put Donald Trump in the White House in the 2016 elections. It is also the primary cause of the dissention of those who believe the ACA is working.

So why exactly was the "Affordable Care Act" so limited in scope and coverage, and why did it not cover everyone the same way it covered the poor?

The answer lies in the current state of the economy, and the failure of a poorly managed and abused welfare system. Either inexpensive, low out of pocket, free market health insurance or a fully tax funded, single payer universal health care plan is only possible when a large portion of the population is working and paying taxes (and/or buying insurance policies.) The reason is that enough funding is required to be able to pay those who are sick. The more people who are not working but who are receiving benefits, the less money there will be in the funds to pay out benefits. The ACA also promotes part time employment over full time. You can't get people, especially single parents, back to work on a part time income – particularly when they also have to pay for their health insurance.

The question of the current state of the U.S. economy is always discussed, but discussions generally fail to sort out exactly why we are in the state we are in, and what can be done to fix it.

Our economy today is far worse than most economists or politicians would have you believe. Taxes are higher than ever, new technology and regulations have imposed significant new costs on us and good jobs are few and far between.

A series of many events has caused a perfect storm of events that has led to high unemployment and underemployment and high cost of living, hurting the middle class American worker the most. In addition, a vast majority of our population is just not in the workforce. In the U.K. and other countries which have universal health care the opposite is true. Virtually every citizen over age 16 is employed.

What are these factors and just how bad is our economy?

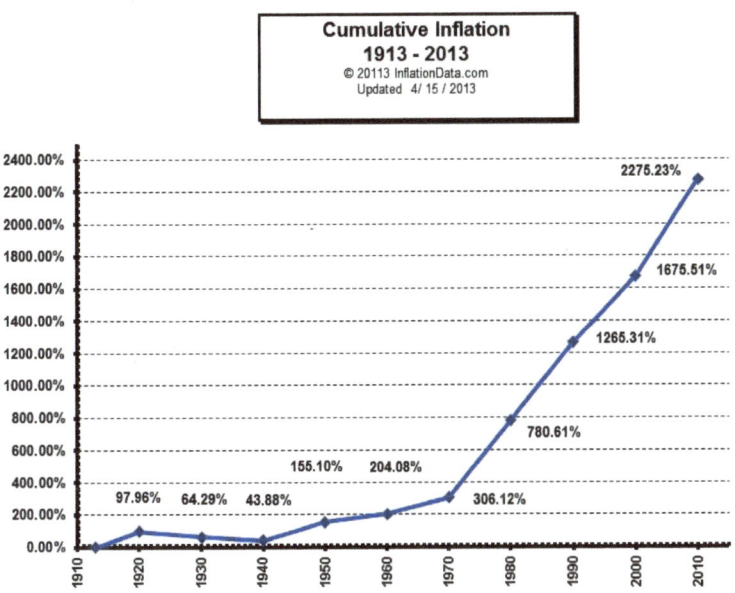

You will notice in this cumulative inflation chart the rise of inflation from 1913-2013. The chart takes a steep climb after 1933 when FDR took the U.S. off the gold standard for domestic trade. You will notice the extreme climb in inflation from 1971 on. In 1971 Richard Nixon stopped the exchange of gold for dollars to foreign countries.

The end of the world gold standard itself is insufficient however to account for our current situation. 1970 Also marked the beginning of a rise to a workforce now consisting of roughly 50 percent woman and a majority of families having 2 or more workers. It also marked the beginning of equal rights for blacks and the start of most of the major entitlement programs – Medicare, Medicaid and others.

The primary factors involved in our economic shift are:

1. The emergence of Women in the workforce
2. Minorities in the workforce
3. Technology stealing jobs
4. Increase in public assistance and disabled workers
5. Increased life expectancy
6. An aging population
7. Decreased tax base due to fewer employed and a shadow economy

Additionally, our modern society and technological advances are adding costs. Plus, the increase in products and services billed on a monthly basis and subscription products is taking money from our paychecks on a regular basis. Then there are new rules, regulations and mandates that did not previously exist.

Chapter Two

Some statistics

U.S. Population as of March 14, 2017
https://www.census.gov/popclock/
323,866,040
There is one birth every 8 seconds
One death every 11 seconds
One international migrant (net) every 32 seconds
Net gain of one person every 15 seconds

% employed in U.S:
73% are either not in the workforce OR are underemployed!
(Not in labor force, underemployed, under age 16)

50% of the current "workforce" is actually employed (and not underemployed!)

(Note – Totals may be off a few percent. Statistics are from those available between 2014 and 2017)

203,387,873 (62.8%) are currently in the workforce (employed or unemployed looking for work, should be working – Does not include those who have given up looking for work)
94,609,000 Not participating in the workforce
103,535,000 Actually employed
5.5% unemployed (in the workforce - can't find work but are looking – this is the statistic you typically hear)
37.4% not in the labor force (included unemployed looking for work or retired)
21.3% on public assistance
13.5% Underemployed
22% (71,006,000) are under age 16 (generally not in the workforce)
6.7% work in a government job, federal/state/local

Record 94,708,000 Americans Not in Labor Force; Participation Rate Drops in May

By Susan Jones | June 3, 2016 | 8:49 AM EDT

(CNSNews.com) - A record 94,708,000 Americans were not in the labor force in May 2016 -- 664,000 more than in April -- and the labor force participation rate dropped two-tenths of a point to 62.6 percent, near its 38-year low, the Labor Department's Bureau of Labor Statistics reported on Friday.

When President Obama took office in January 2009, 80,529,000 Americans were not participating in the labor force; since then, 14,179,000 Americans have left the workforce -- some of them retiring and some just quitting because they can't find work.

Underemployed:
https://www.statista.com/statistics/205240/us-underemployment-rate/
13.5% March 2017

On public assistance:
https://www.census.gov/newsroom/press-releases/2015/cb15-97.html
21.3% of US Participates in Government Assistance Programs

Civilian Employees:
103,535,000 Civilian employees as of April, 2017

Of those employed:
There were 21,995,000 employed by federal, state and local government in the United States in August, 2016, according to the Bureau of Labor Statistics. By contrast, there were only 12,329,000 employed in the manufacturing sector as of April 2017

Total employed as of April 2017:
103,535,000

JAPAN

The labor force in Japan numbered 65.9 million people in 2010, which was 59.6% of the population of 15 years old and older, and amongst them, 62.57 million people were employed, whereas 3.34 million people were unemployed which made the unemployment rate 5.1%. --- 95% of the Japanese workforce is employed!

https://en.wikipedia.org/wiki/Labor_market_of_Japan

Great Depression Era Unemployment Statistics

Year	Population	Unemployed
1932	91,810,000	12,060,000
1933	92,950,000	12,830,000
1934	94,190,000	11,340,000

12% of population not working! (25.2% of total workforce, which was 52% of the population)

Table 1.
Population by Sex and Selected Age Groups: 2000 and 2010
(For information on confidentiality protection, nonsampling error, and definitions, see *www.census.gov/prod/cen2010/doc/sf1.pdf*)

Sex and selected age groups	2000		2010		Change, 2000 to 2010	
	Number	Percent	Number	Percent	Number	Percent
Total population	281,421,906	100.0	308,745,538	100.0	27,323,632	9.7
SEX						
Male...........................	138,053,563	49.1	151,781,326	49.2	13,727,763	9.9
Female.........................	143,368,343	50.9	156,964,212	50.8	13,595,869	9.5
SELECTED AGE GROUPS						
Under 18 years	72,293,812	25.7	74,181,467	24.0	1,887,655	2.6
Under 5 years	19,175,798	6.8	20,201,362	6.5	1,025,564	5.3
5 to 17 years	53,118,014	18.9	53,980,105	17.5	862,091	1.6
18 to 44 years	112,183,705	39.9	112,806,642	36.5	622,937	0.6
18 to 24 years	27,143,454	9.5	30,672,088	9.9	3,528,634	13.0
25 to 44 years	85,040,251	30.2	82,134,554	26.6	−2,905,697	−3.4
45 to 64 years	61,952,636	22.0	81,489,445	26.4	19,536,809	31.5
65 years and over	34,991,753	12.4	40,267,984	13.0	5,276,231	15.1
16 years and over	217,149,127	77.2	243,275,505	78.8	26,126,378	12.0
18 years and over	209,128,094	74.3	234,564,071	76.0	25,435,977	12.2
21 years and over	196,899,193	70.0	220,958,853	71.6	24,059,660	12.2
62 years and over	41,256,029	14.7	49,972,181	16.2	8,716,152	21.1

Sources: U.S. Census Bureau, *Census 2000 Summary File 1* and *2010 Census Summary File 1.*

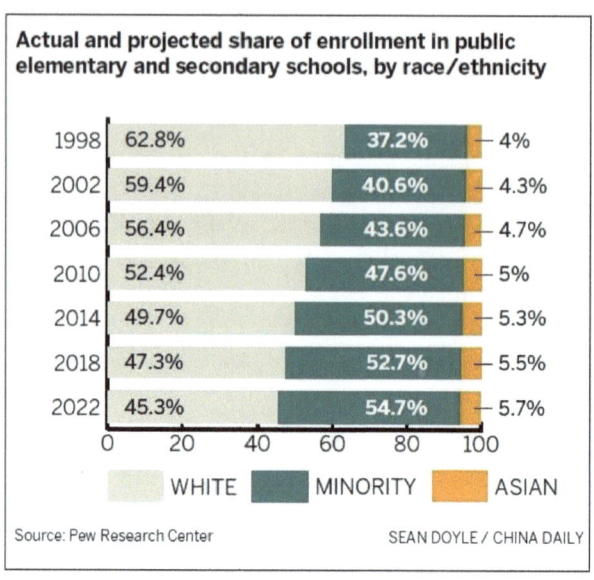

Actual and projected share of enrollment in public elementary and secondary schools, by race/ethnicity

Year	WHITE	MINORITY	ASIAN
1998	62.8%	37.2%	4%
2002	59.4%	40.6%	4.3%
2006	56.4%	43.6%	4.7%
2010	52.4%	47.6%	5%
2014	49.7%	50.3%	5.3%
2018	47.3%	52.7%	5.5%
2022	45.3%	54.7%	5.7%

Source: Pew Research Center

SEAN DOYLE / CHINA DAILY

Data extracted on: May 10, 2017 (11:20:32 AM)

Labor Force Statistics from the Current Population Survey

```
Series Id:           LNS11300000
Seasonally Adjusted
Series title:        (Seas) Labor Force Participation Rate
Labor force status:  Civilian labor force participation rate
Type of data:        Percent or rate
Age:                 16 years and over
```

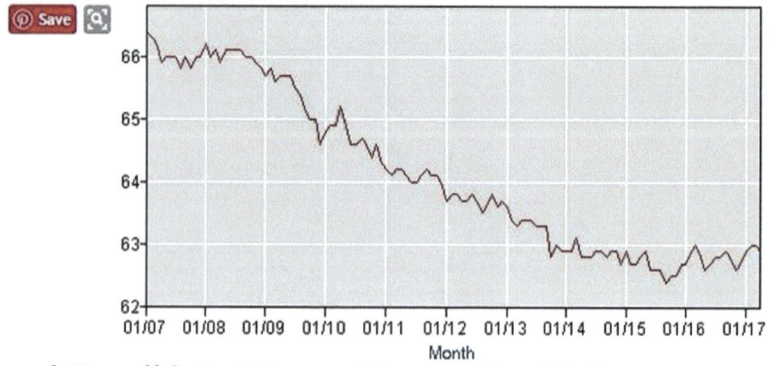

https://data.bls.gov/timeseries/LNS11300000

18

Chapter Three
The issues

Women in the workforce:

Women traditionally during our nations' early years were few in the workplace. As the 20th century progressed, women began making inroads in the workplace and have gained virtual equality, though still are paid less than men in many cases. Capitalists and business executives have taken notice, and now look at the family unit as typically consisting of 2 workers... or more. Today, the number of men v/s women in the workforce is almost equal, and costs have gone up accordingly. Since the average family unit now earns double what it did in the past, prices have pretty much doubled! Businesses base their pricing on total family income. Thus, we now work twice as hard for half as much.

Minorities in the workforce:

Minorities in the workforce have increased and anti-discrimination and equality laws are now in place. This increases the available workforce, but good paying jobs are at a premium since now you have both women and minorities added to the previously white male workforce. Consequently, it is a "buyers' market" where business can pay less because there is more demand and fewer jobs.

Technology and automation:

Technology and automation will claim over 40% of all available jobs by 2030 according to "Forbes" magazine. This will force more people into retirement and more out of the workforce or into a job that pays less than a sustainable income.

As Carl Marx said over 100 years ago in his "Manifesto of the Communist Regime" "The advance of industry, whose involuntary promoter is the capitalist, replaces the isolation of the laborers, due to competition, by their revolutionary combination, due to association. The development of modern industry, therefore, cuts from under its feet the very foundation on which the capitalist produces and appropriates products. What the capitalist, therefore, produces, above all, is its own grave-diggers. Its fall and the victory of the laborers are equally inevitable."

Essentially the industrial revolution and new technologies kill the very industries they created.

The aging population:

The "baby boomers" are retiring at an alarming rate, and in 15 years virtually every "boomer" will be of retirement age, and many will be forced out of the workforce. Many will be retiring at poverty levels and will end up on public assistance. The reduced workforce will be unable to sustain these additional people.

Some random thoughts:

If you look at the historic data you will find that the various charts of wages, inflation, value of the dollar, etc. correlate directly with national events. Some have been already noted, but others follow.

1. The dropping of the gold standard: June 1933 FDR took the U.S. off the gold standard which had been in place since 1879. He recalled all gold held by private individuals. The U.S. continued to allow foreign governments to exchange dollars for gold until 1971, when President Richard Nixon abruptly ended the practice to stop dollar-flush foreigners from sapping U.S. gold reserves.

2. Taxation. As the workforce decreases, tax revenue significantly decreases, demanding increases in taxation. There is a breaking point to all this. This is a point somewhere between 0% (no taxation of income) and 100% (obviously it is not feasible to tax someone 100% of their income.) This was explained best by the Laffer curve (named after Arthur Laffer who first described the

ideal amount that one could be taxed to provide maximum revenue.) There have been studies showing that higher taxes don't always bring in higher revenue. When taxes reach the "breaking point" there is less compliance and more avoidance of paying the high tax. Additionally, more and more items are being taxed, and like a million paper cuts can kill, so can many small taxes.

3. Laws and mandates. Many new laws are in place than we had 20 or 30 years ago. These laws force companies and individuals to comply with various regulations that can directly or indirectly cost a considerable sum of money. An example would be automobile manufacturing regulations. While our regulations increase gas mileage and safety, they cost the consumer a significant amount of money. Rules to keep wastewater clean sound good, but they are unfunded, and costs are passed to the consumer as rate increases.

4. New technologies. These days we are forced to pay for many new technologies that we did not have to pay for in the past. The ubiquitous mobile phone is a virtual necessity these days, and one cannot get very far without Internet access. Even most television is now consumed over a cable, costing hundreds of dollars a month sometimes. Also, many online and other services are offered only on a monthly payment basis – they can no longer be bought outright. Even National Geographic magazine has to be purchased monthly with online content at a cost twice as much as the print version used to be!

5. Inflation. While inflation typically follows increases in prosperity, we are now seeing the bulk of that prosperity going to the corporations as profit due primarily to automation. Every employee hired today is able to do the work that up to 10 employees used to do. Productivity is way up, prices and cost of services have gone up but employee wages have remained stagnant and have even gone down. Job growth has significantly decreased.

6. Public assistance. The increase in public assistance needs to be paid for by the remaining workers, who are fewer and fewer every day.

7. Part time employment. Large companies should be penalized for hiring part time workers and should be rewarded for hiring full time. It is not possible to get people (single parents in

particular) off public assistance when only part time jobs are available. The cost of child care, health insurance, etc. would exceed the income earned at their job.
8. The Shadow Economy. Loss of tax base and revenue due to untaxed online sales, underground cash sales, illicit drug sales and other unreported income.

Chapter Four

Effects of our current economic state

1. We have a serious socio-political divide in our country. There are many polarizing issues, but to sum up in general the right wants smaller government, fewer regulations and a self-regulating economy. The left wants more social services, more dependence on government, more government control and government control of our money and resources. The problem is that with only 27 percent of the U.S. population working neither free market nor universal healthcare can work! This is one reason that the Affordable Care Act came into being, and is the major reason it is failing. In reality we should have one of two choices. Either we have a fully self-regulating healthcare industry, where supply and demand and ability to pay control cost, or we have a fully social, universal healthcare plan paid for out of government funding paid for by our taxes. With the former, the costs can only be controlled by having a large percentage of the population paying for their insurance out of pocket. For the latter, you need a large tax base consisting of a majority of able bodied people working and paying taxes. We have neither – We only have 27 percent of our entire population working. As far as healthcare? We ended up the worst possible healthcare plan, "Obamacare." Since there are not enough people working to pay for the plan, the plan robs from the already strained middle class worker by overcharging for insurance and by placing unreasonable out of pocket costs on their insurance. The plan gives free or dirt cheap insurance with virtually no deductibles or out of pocket costs to the poor and to the most costly constituents – those with high cost preexisting conditions. Is it any wonder that the middle class stood up in the 2016 elections and said "Enough already!" Is it really any wonder how Donald Trump ended up in the White House, preaching that he will eliminate this terrible, discriminatory program?

2. Healthcare is but one program that is affected by a non-working population. Costs for everything go up. Why tax cigarettes and liquor? It is one way to tax the poor, who are more prone to abuse of these vices. Why sell lottery tickets, and tax casinos?

Again, this is one of the few ways to tax the poor, who are playing the games to try and get out of poverty. Why raise the gasoline tax? With fewer people in the workforce to pay taxes, there is no money to repair our infrastructure. This goes on and on, but without working people to pay taxes and to buy products and services costs for everyone will go up.

3. Workers working harder. With fewer people working or willing to work those remaining in the work force end up doing "double duty," working harder to produce the same output of labor.

4. Finally, when one discusses the causes of our situation the facts listed above come into play, and the left will deem those who promote these causes as misogynistic, racist or as white supremacists, when in reality the facts speak for themselves. The problem is that we need to stop speaking in terms of sex, gender and race, and start thinking of people as just "people." We need to count heads and count jobs, count the working and the non-working, and seek the reasons why people are not working or are underemployed and correct those issues. The future of everyone is at stake and we need to chart a path to the future that works for everyone.

_____

_____

_____

Chapter Five

The solution?

1. Reform the welfare system! Step one is to get everyone off welfare that does not truly belong on it. Get them back in the workforce to help pay for our programs and debt. Get any and all illegals off ALL welfare and public assistance programs.
2. Encourage businesses to hire full time, penalize part time job creation.
3. LOWER the retirement age – this will open more jobs for the next generation and reduce unemployment. Pay for this by removing the social security tax cap – why is this capped in the first place, and why at such a low dollar amount? Increase social security benefit payments to encourage retirement from the workforce.
4. Provide incentive for businesses to locate and remain in the U.S., and to hire and keep U.S. citizens in the workforce. Penalize those who locate offshore or hire offshore or non-citizen staff.
5. Combine public welfare agencies and staff into one plan with varying benefits.
6. Combine taxes. Why are there so many taxes to begin with? It seems to me that we are paying tax on our taxes these days. Would it not be more cost effective to eliminate ALL taxes and have just ONE federal and ONE state tax? (The states would collect and pay the municipalities and schools the tax they normally would collect.)
7. Increase online sales tax compliance.
8. Change taxing in such a way that even money from unreported income is taxed.
9. Other ideas??

This document is meant to be a starting point to understanding the situation we are currently in. It is not intended to offer all the solutions. One of the greatest problems today is that both the right and the left as well as all those in between think that you can magically enact just about anything. This is far from the truth. With the ACA for example you see those who are happy getting free medical care (they essentially HAVE the universal healthcare that everyone else seems to want) and those facing bankruptcy over a $10,000.00 hospital bill. No, the plan not only does not work, but it can't work. Only the insurance companies, hospitals, pharmaceutical companies and lawyers are benefitting from this plan. The underlying system needs to be fixed before we can move forward!

Chapter Six

The charts!

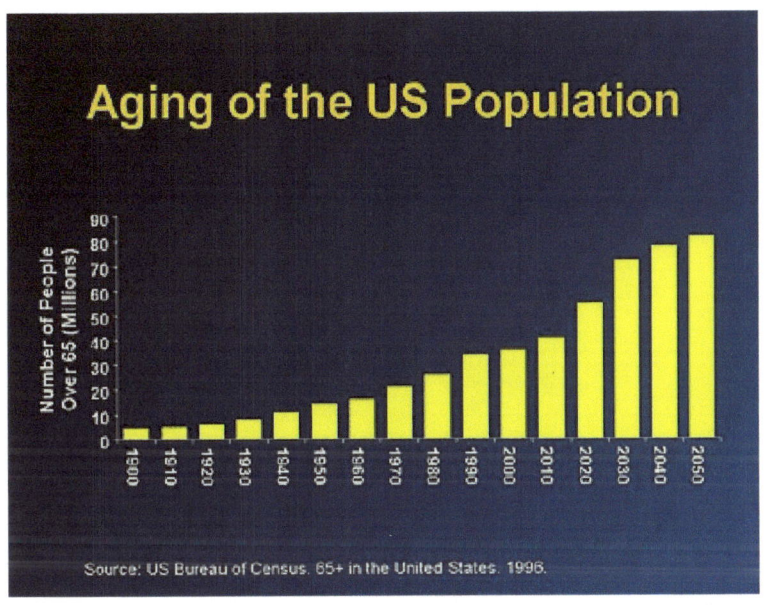

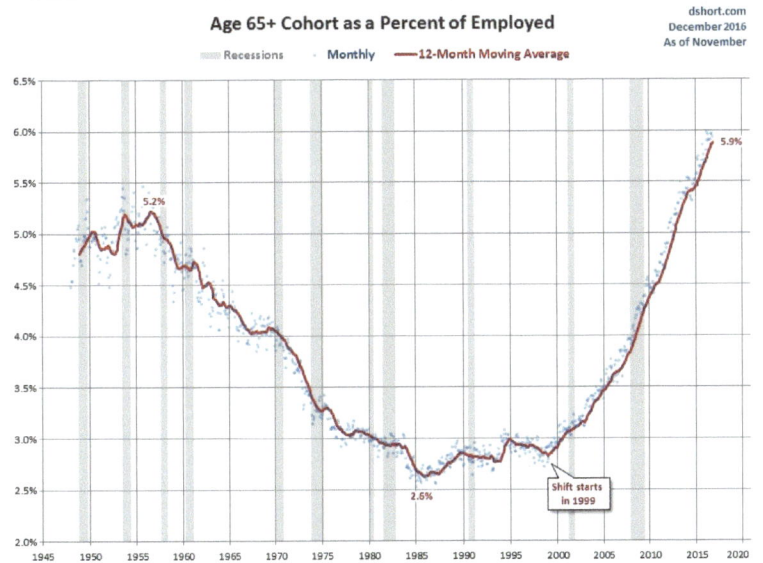

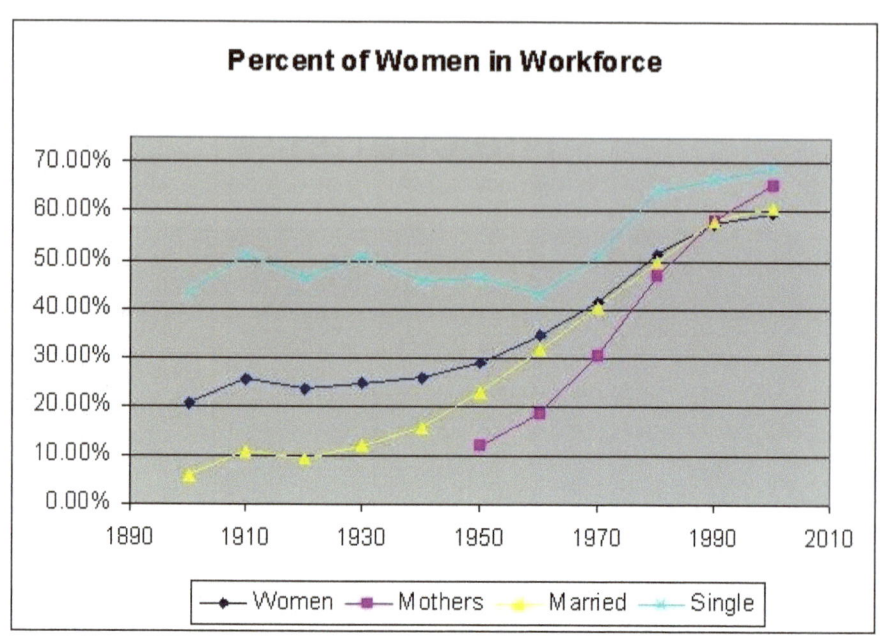

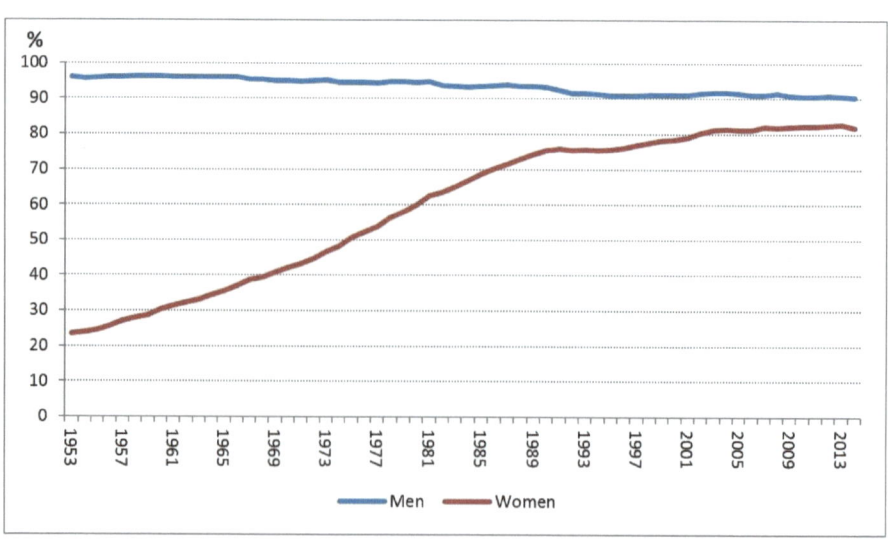

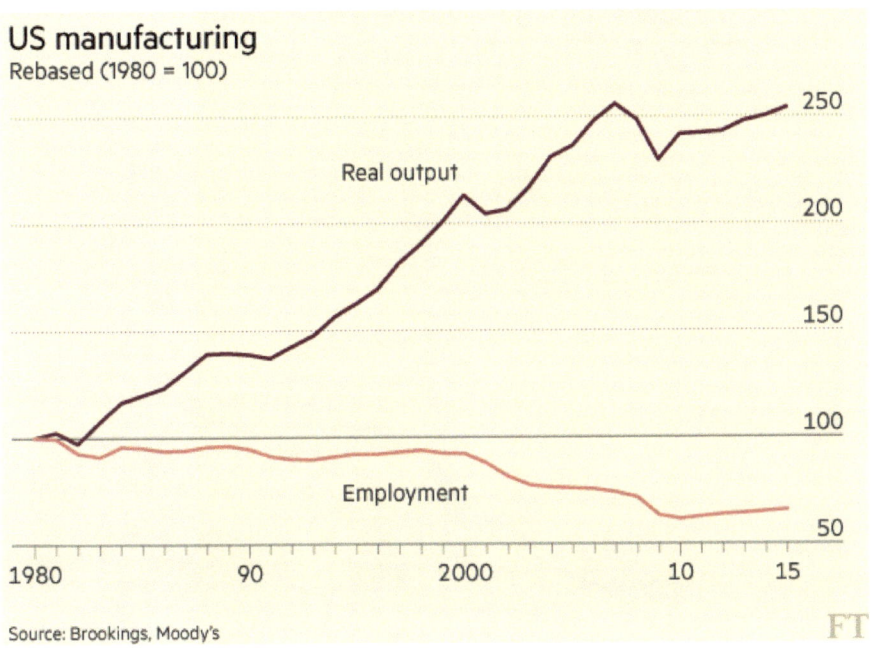

US manufacturing
Rebased (1980 = 100)

Real output

Employment

1980 · 90 · 2000 · 10 · 15

250
200
150
100
50

Source: Brookings, Moody's

FT

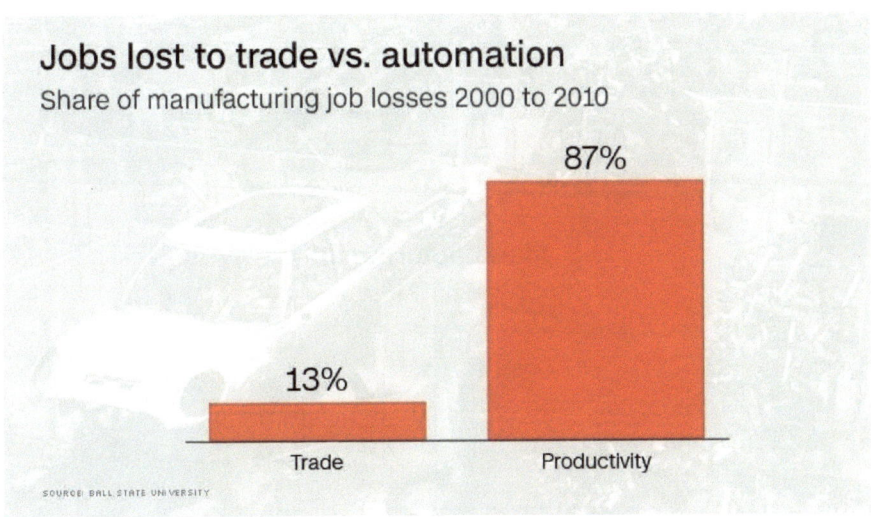

Jobs lost to trade vs. automation
Share of manufacturing job losses 2000 to 2010

13% Trade
87% Productivity

SOURCE: BALL STATE UNIVERSITY

U.S. Manufacturing Productivity and Ouput Have Risen While Employment Has Declined

1987=100%

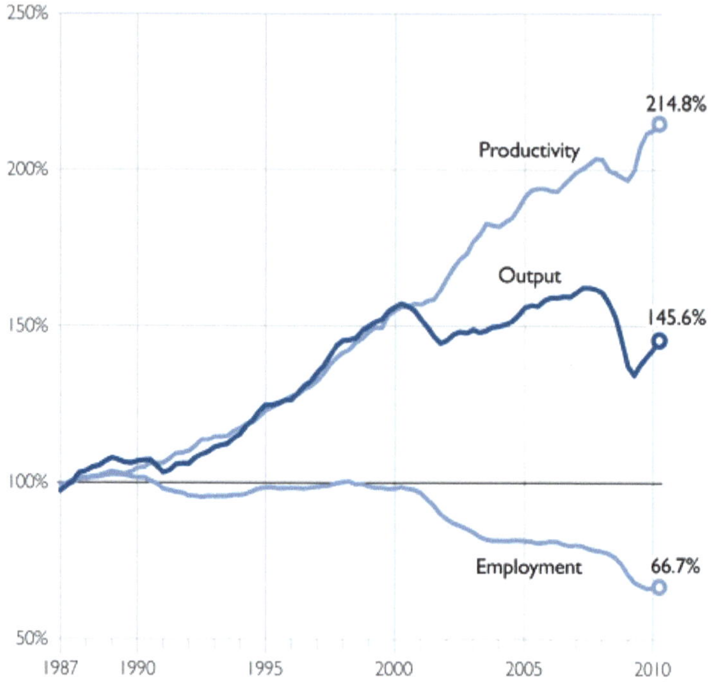

Productivity 214.8%

Output

145.6%

Employment 66.7%

Source: U.S. Department of Labor, Bureau of Labor Statistics, "Productivity and Costs: Manufacturing Sector," 1987–2010, in Data Link Express, Haver Analytics.

Chart 5 • B 2476 ☎ heritage.org

U.S. Manufacturing Jobs

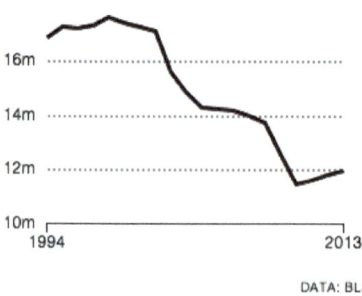

DATA: BLS

Decoupling Productivity and Employment

Digital technologies have boosted productivity in the United States without also spurring the expected job growth, argue Erik Brynjolfsson and Andrew McAfee. A result of this decoupling is that while gross domestic product (GDP) has risen, median income has not, and inequality has grown.

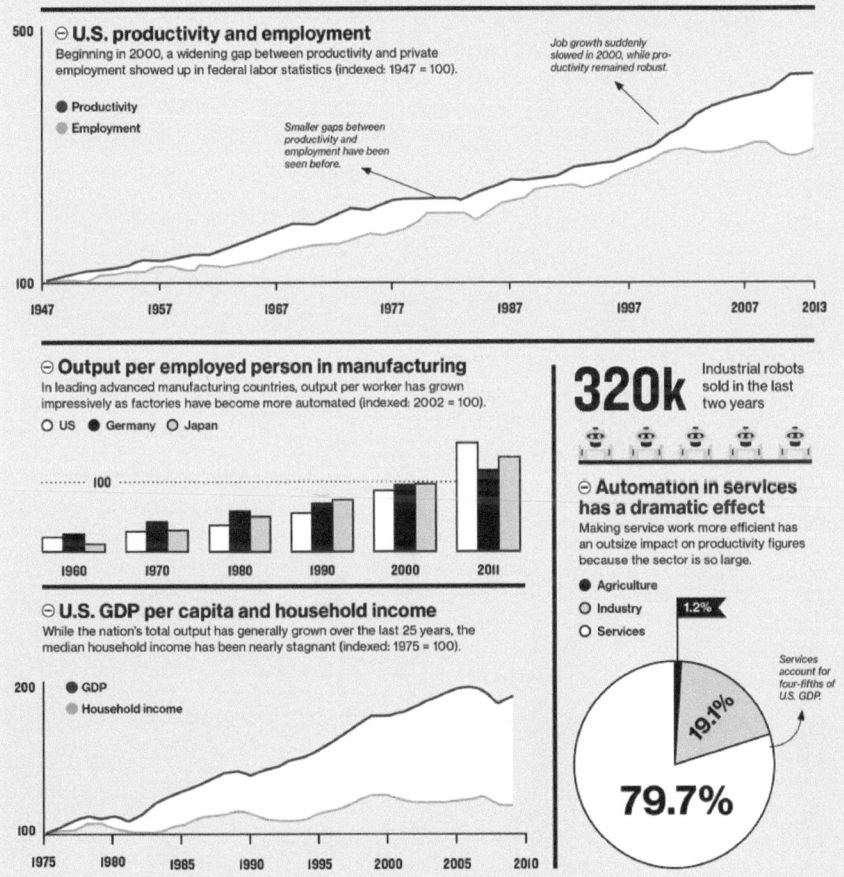

⊖ U.S. productivity and employment

Beginning in 2000, a widening gap between productivity and private employment showed up in federal labor statistics (indexed: 1947 = 100).

● Productivity
● Employment

Smaller gaps between productivity and employment have been seen before.

Job growth suddenly slowed in 2000, while productivity remained robust.

500 — 100
1947 1957 1967 1977 1987 1997 2007 2013

⊖ Output per employed person in manufacturing

In leading advanced manufacturing countries, output per worker has grown impressively as factories have become more automated (indexed: 2002 = 100).

○ US ● Germany ○ Japan

100

1960 1970 1980 1990 2000 2011

⊖ U.S. GDP per capita and household income

While the nation's total output has generally grown over the last 25 years, the median household income has been nearly stagnant (indexed: 1975 = 100).

● GDP
● Household income

200 — 100
1975 1980 1985 1990 1995 2000 2005 2010

320k

Industrial robots sold in the last two years

⊖ Automation in services has a dramatic effect

Making service work more efficient has an outsize impact on productivity figures because the sector is so large.

● Agriculture
○ Industry
○ Services

1.2%
19.1%
79.7%

Services account for four-fifths of U.S. GDP.

31

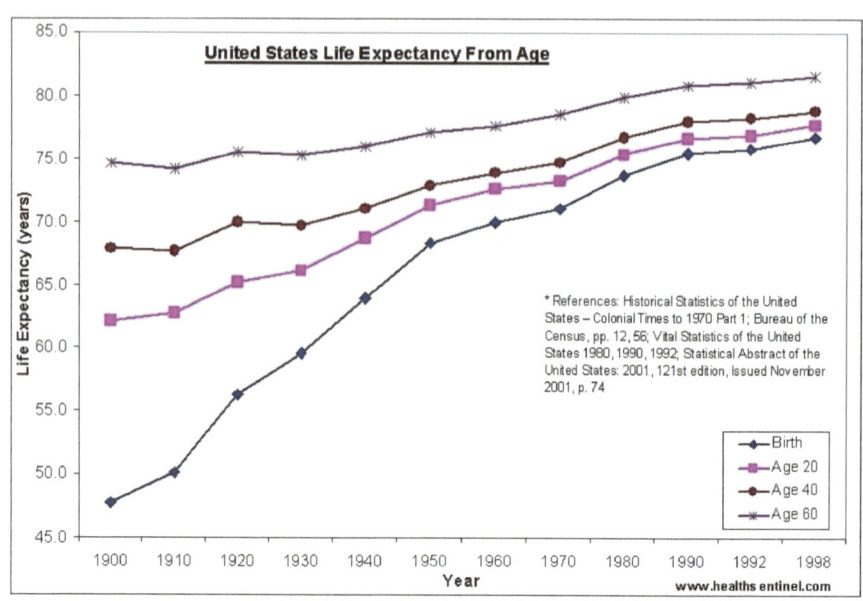

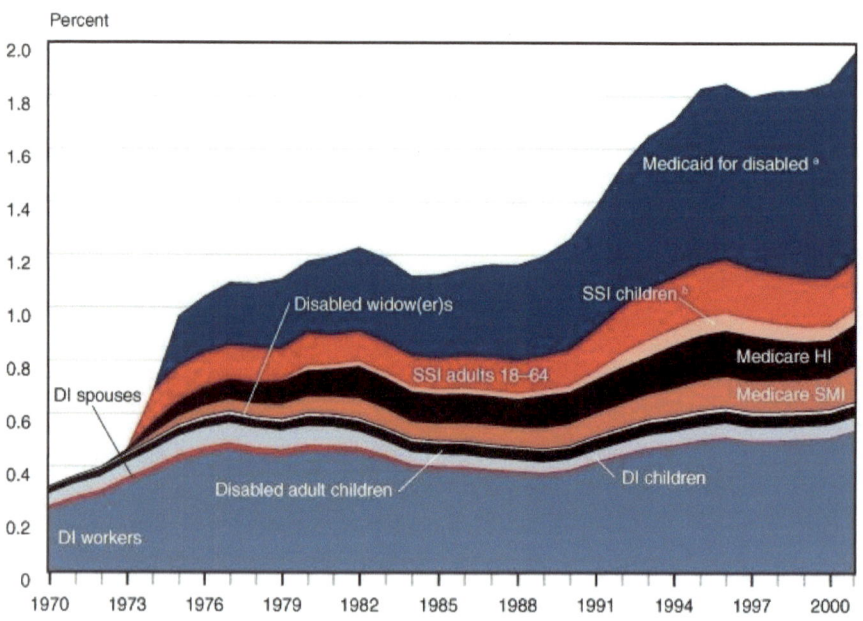

32

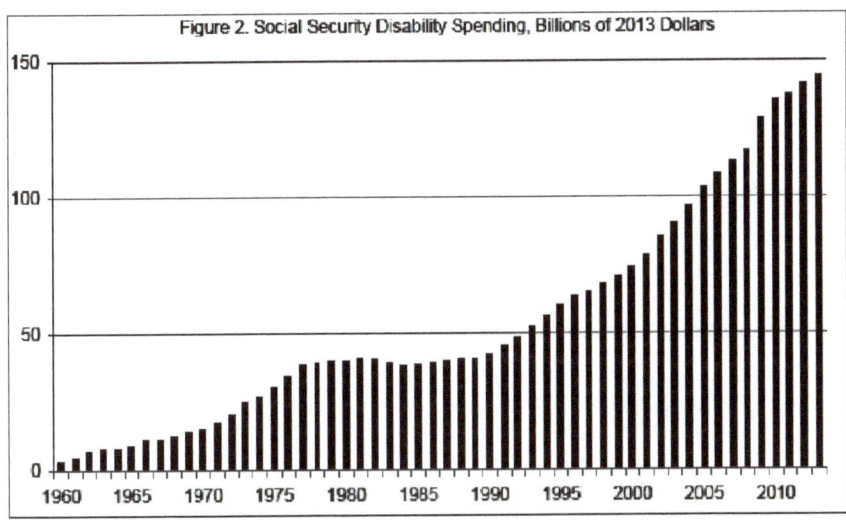

Figure 2. Social Security Disability Spending, Billions of 2013 Dollars

Source: *Budget of the U.S. Government, Fiscal Year 2014, Historical Tables*, Table 13.1. Fiscal years.

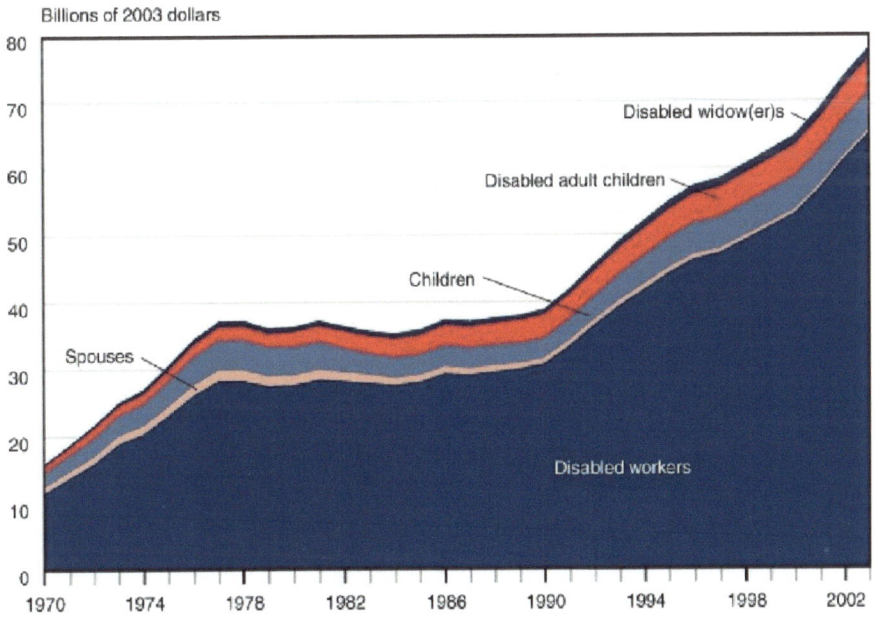

33

Share Of Newly Disabled Workers, By Diagnosis

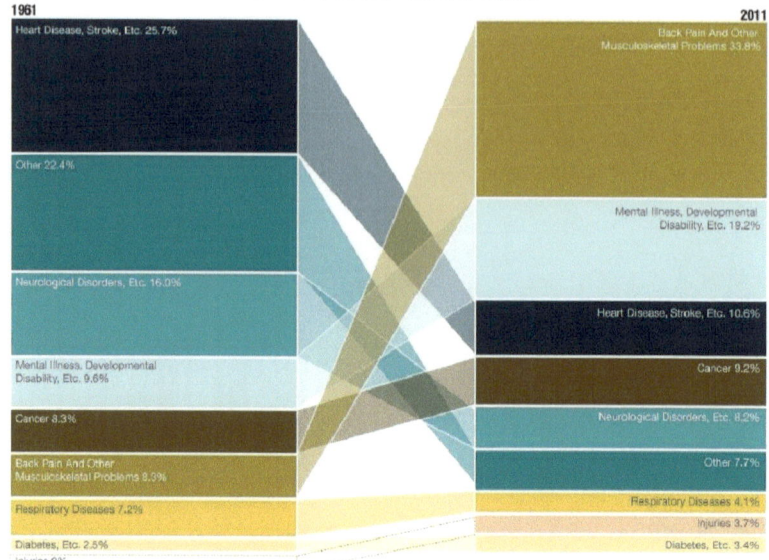

1961

Heart Disease, Stroke, Etc. 25.7%

Other 22.4%

Neurological Disorders, Etc. 16.0%

Mental Illness, Developmental Disability, Etc. 9.6%

Cancer 8.3%

Back Pain And Other Musculoskeletal Problems 8.3%

Respiratory Diseases 7.2%

Diabetes, Etc. 2.5%

Injuries 0%

2011

Back Pain And Other Musculoskeletal Problems 33.8%

Mental Illness, Developmental Disability, Etc. 19.2%

Heart Disease, Stroke, Etc. 10.6%

Cancer 9.2%

Neurological Disorders, Etc. 8.2%

Other 7.7%

Respiratory Diseases 4.1%

Injuries 3.7%

Diabetes, Etc. 3.4%

As The Number Of Families On Welfare Declined ...

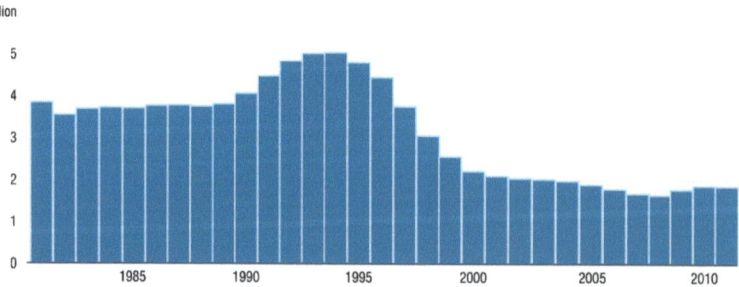

6 Million

... The Number Of Low-Income People On Disability Rose

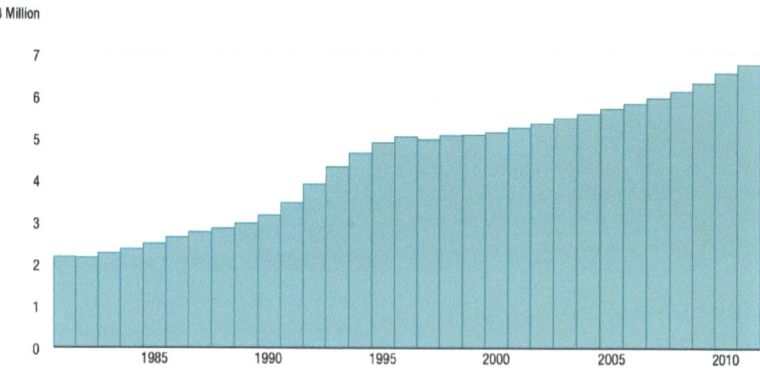

8 Million

34

U.S. Employment Trends

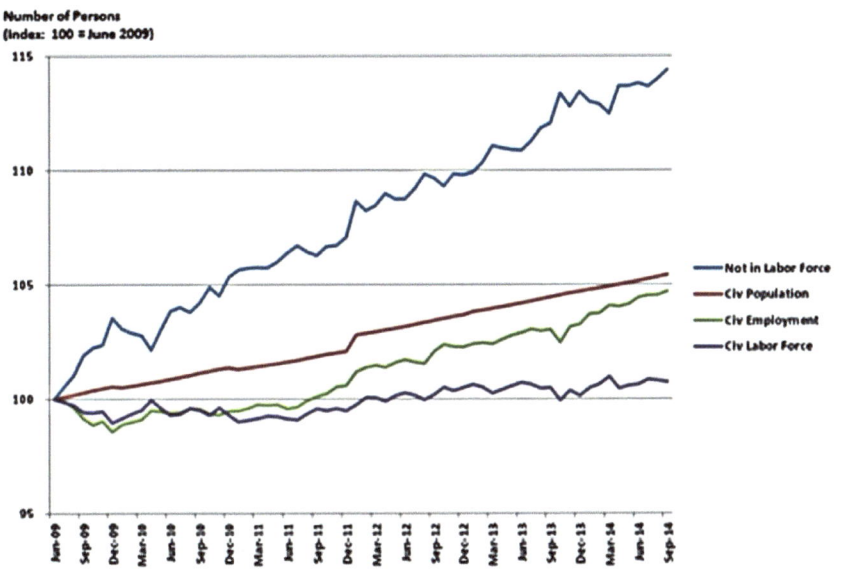

Number of Persons
(Index: 100 = June 2009)

Legend:
- Not in Labor Force
- Civ Population
- Civ Employment
- Civ Labor Force

Source Data: Federal Reserve Database (FRED)
Not in labor force = Civilian Population – Civilian Labor Force

FRED

— Compensation of employees: Wages and salaries/Gross Domestic Product*100
— Civilian Employment-Population Ratio

Shaded areas indicate US recessions - 2015 research.stlouisfed.org

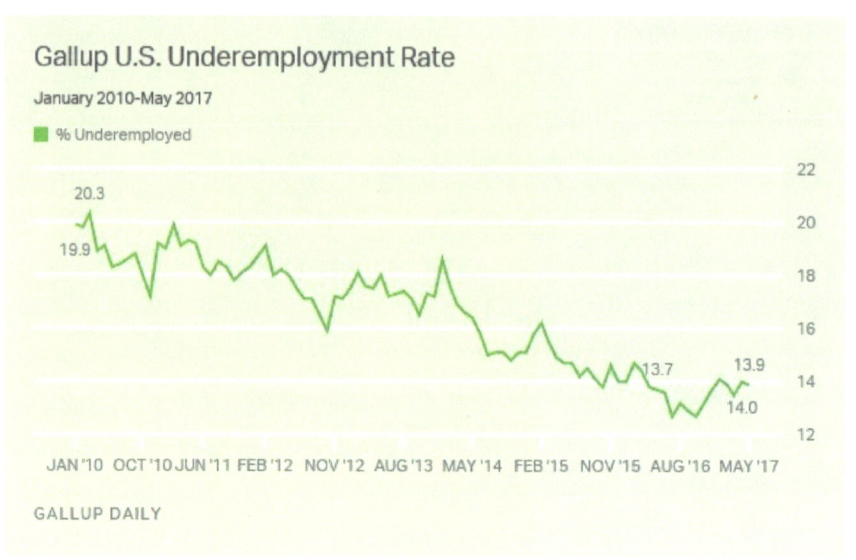

Gallup U.S. Underemployment Rate

January 2010-May 2017

■ % Underemployed

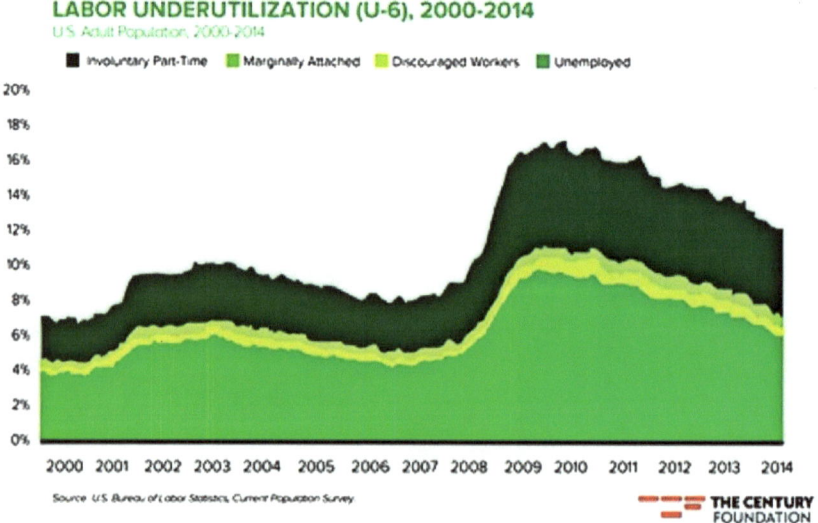

LABOR UNDERUTILIZATION (U-6), 2000-2014

U.S. Adult Population, 2000-2014

■ Involuntary Part-Time ■ Marginally Attached ■ Discouraged Workers ■ Unemployed

Source: U.S. Bureau of Labor Statistics, Current Population Survey

THE CENTURY FOUNDATION

The Laffer Curve

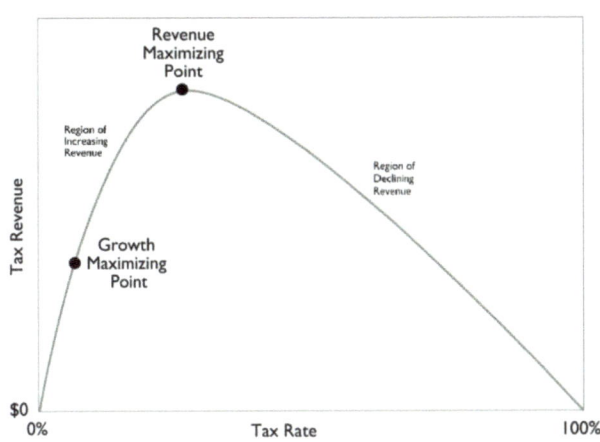

Projected U.S. Population Growth

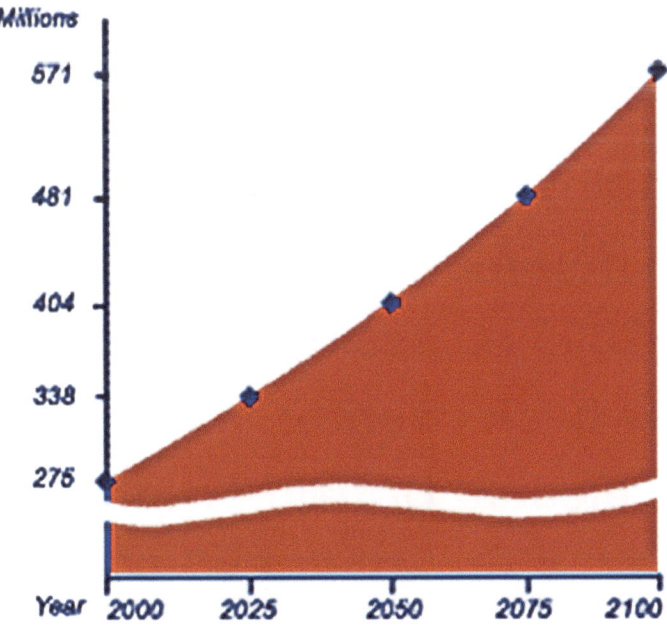

Data: U.S. Census Bureau

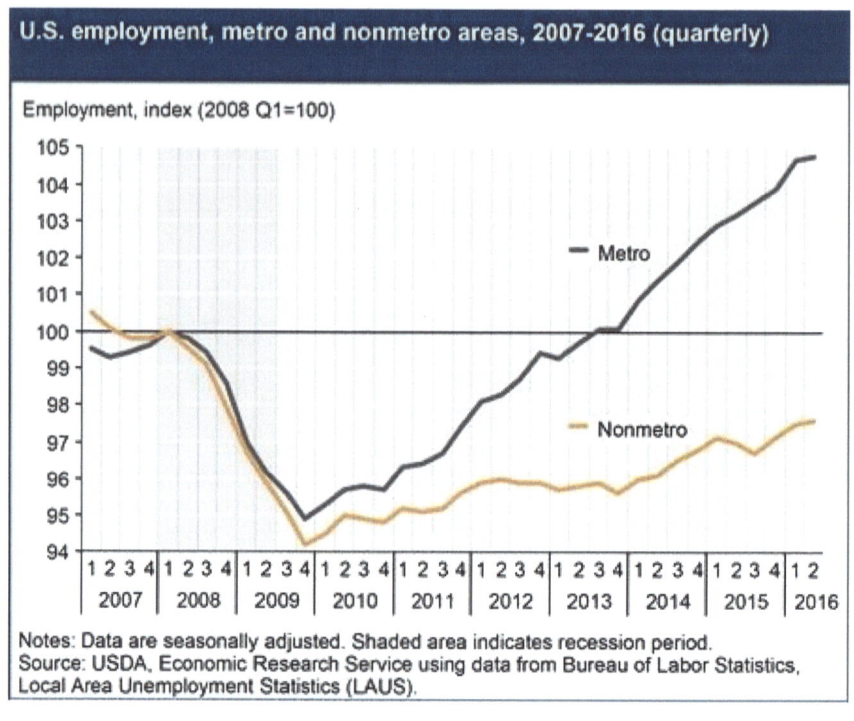

U.S. employment, metro and nonmetro areas, 2007-2016 (quarterly)

Employment, index (2008 Q1=100)

— Metro

— Nonmetro

| 1 2 3 4 | 1 2 3 4 | 1 2 3 4 | 1 2 3 4 | 1 2 3 4 | 1 2 3 4 | 1 2 3 4 | 1 2 3 4 | 1 2 3 4 | 1 2 |
| 2007 | 2008 | 2009 | 2010 | 2011 | 2012 | 2013 | 2014 | 2015 | 2016 |

Notes: Data are seasonally adjusted. Shaded area indicates recession period.
Source: USDA, Economic Research Service using data from Bureau of Labor Statistics,
Local Area Unemployment Statistics (LAUS).

Employment never recovered in the non-metropolitan areas after the 2008 recession. Any idea why the back country rebelled and elected Donald Trump??

Chapter Seven
The shadow economy

What Is the Shadow Economy and Why Does It Matter?

Unlicensed construction or illegal sales by food vendors—it all has an impact on the real economy

By

Simon Constable, The Wall Street Journal

Updated March 5, 2017 11:33 p.m. ET

The shadow economy is perhaps best described by the activities of those operating in it: work done for cash, where taxes aren't paid and regulations aren't strictly followed.

Most of the businesses operating in the shadow economy aren't what most people would think of as criminal enterprises, says Cristina Terra, professor of economics at Essec Business School in France, and author of the book "Principles of International Finance and Open Economy Macroeconomics."

"Those involved aren't paying taxes, but they are typically producing goods that formal firms would produce," she says. Such activities could include unlicensed construction or illegal sales by food vendors.

The size of this sector of the economy has grown large in some countries.

"As a percentage of GDP, it ranges from 25-60% in South America, [and] from 13-50% in Asia," according to a recent paper by Prof. Terra.

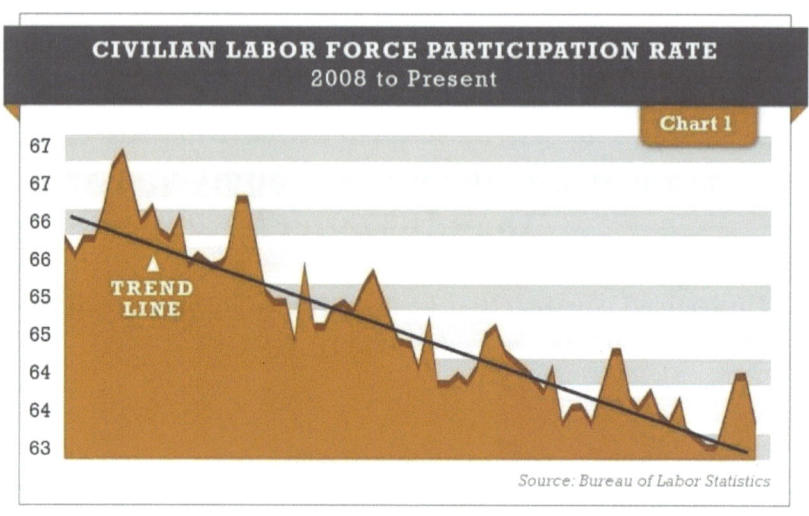

CIVILIAN LABOR FORCE PARTICIPATION RATE
2008 to Present

Chart 1

67
67
66
66
65
65
64
64
63

▲ TREND LINE

Source: *Bureau of Labor Statistics*

Reasons for the existence of a shadow economy, and its structure

Reasons for the existence of a shadow economy:

1. To avoid payment of taxes or surcharges. This is caused by excessive taxation or an excessively complex system of taxation.
2. To avoid payment of Social Security, Medicare, and other social welfare payments.
3. To circumvent labor laws, including minimum wage, hours and safety standards.
4. To avoid the complexity of operating a legal business.
5. To save on costs when total annual transactions are minimal.

Structure:

Legal Activities:

1. Unreported income from self-employment related to otherwise legal services, such as flea market sales, barter, online sales.
2. Employee perks and fringe benefits not reported.
3. Handyman and do-it-yourself work.

Illegal Activities:

1. Trade in stolen goods
2. Illicit drug dealing
3. Prostitution
4. Gambling
5. Smuggling
6. Fraud
7. Theft

In the U.S. the shadow economy equates to about $1 Billion dollars

(The KNOWN amount, surely it is far larger!)

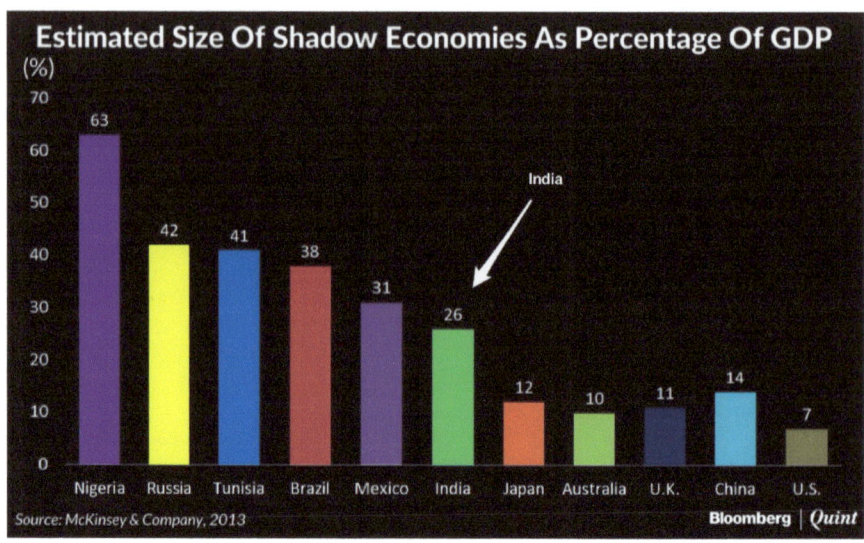

Estimated Size Of Shadow Economies As Percentage Of GDP

Source: McKinsey & Company, 2013

Bloomberg | Quint

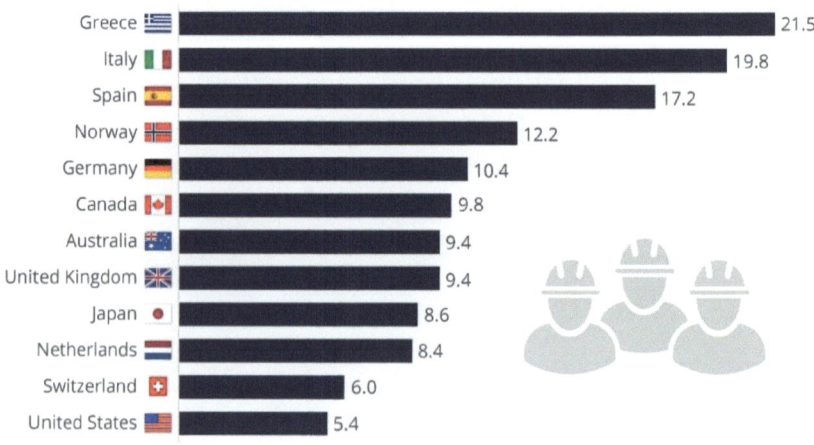

Where Shadow Economies Are Well Established

Shadow economy as a percentage of GDP in selected countries (2017)*

Greece	21.5
Italy	19.8
Spain	17.2
Norway	12.2
Germany	10.4
Canada	9.8
Australia	9.4
United Kingdom	9.4
Japan	8.6
Netherlands	8.4
Switzerland	6.0
United States	5.4

Shadow economy is the part of an economy involving goods and services which are paid for in cash, not declared for tax and therefore not actually part of the GDP

@StatistaCharts   Source: IAW

Forbes statista

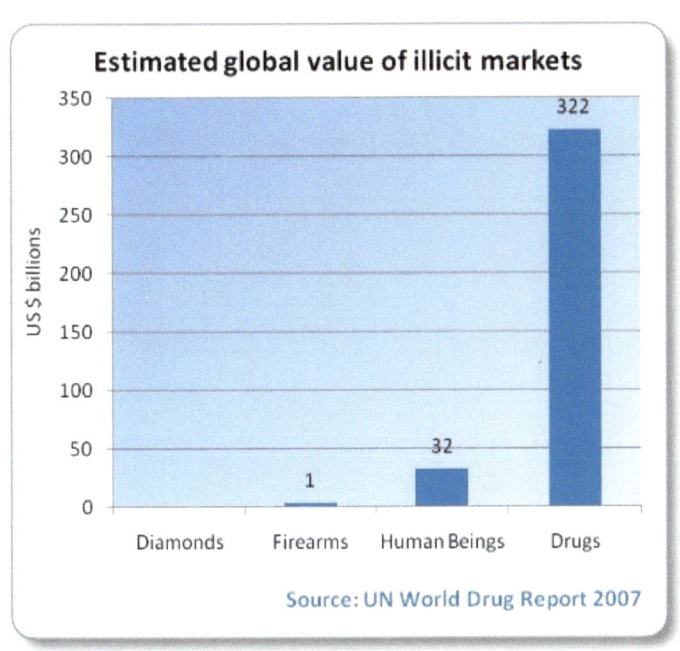

Estimated global value of illicit markets

Source: UN World Drug Report 2007

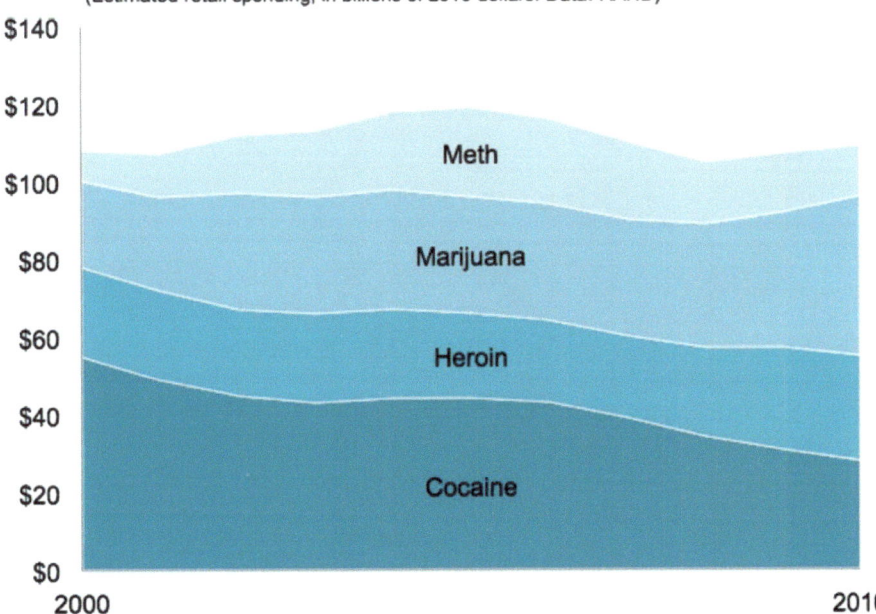

What America Spends On Drugs
(Estimated retail spending, in billions of 2010 dollars. Data: RAND)

43

Chapter Eight
The case for universal healthcare

The cost of universal, single payer healthcare was calculated and presented by Senator Bernie Sanders in 2016. Even if you consider overruns and additional costs that many economists have predicted the total cost over 11 years would be approximately $57.4 Trillion ($5.7 Trillion per year.) This compares to our current healthcare expenditures of $2.6 Trillion per year. The cost of universal healthcare is thus about twice our current cost – which just so happens to coincide with the number of unemployed who could be working! Get the people back to work and we can implement any health insurance plan we want!

Naysayers will say that Universal Healthcare is too costly. What they neglect to consider is the current cost of Medicare, Medicaid, VA health, etc. If Universal Healthcare were implemented, all of these programs and their infrastructure would vanish, and the plan could pay for itself at current funding rates. The problem is that the health insurance industry, along with all their lobbyists would also disappear... Therein lies the problem! These same lobbyists control the politicians' purse strings.

National Health Expenditures in the United States, by Source of Payment, 2010

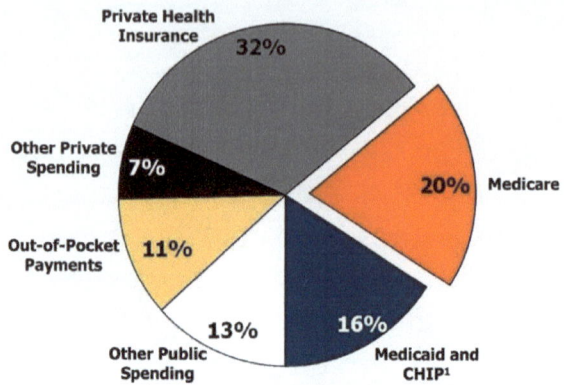

Private Health Insurance 32%

Other Private Spending 7%

Out-of-Pocket Payments 11%

13% **Other Public Spending**

16% **Medicaid and CHIP[1]**

20% **Medicare**

Total National Health Expenditures, 2010 = $2.6 Trillion

NOTES: [1]Includes Children's Health Insurance Program (CHIP) and Children's Health Insurance Program expansion (Title XIX).
SOURCE: Centers for Medicare & Medicaid Services, Office of the Actuary, National Health Expenditure Projections 2009-2019, February 2010.

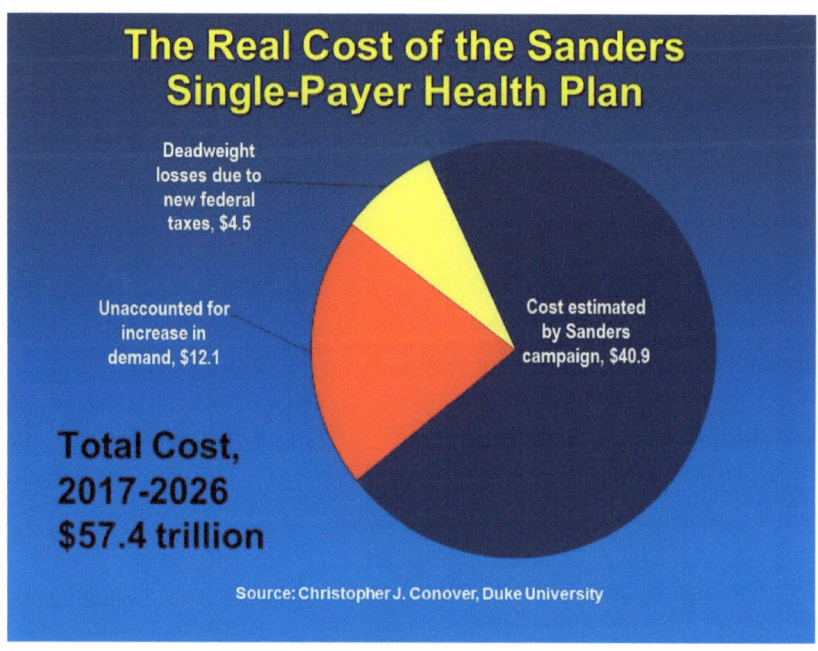

The Real Cost of the Sanders Single-Payer Health Plan

Deadweight losses due to new federal taxes, $4.5

Unaccounted for increase in demand, $12.1

Cost estimated by Sanders campaign, $40.9

Total Cost, 2017-2026 $57.4 trillion

Source: Christopher J. Conover, Duke University

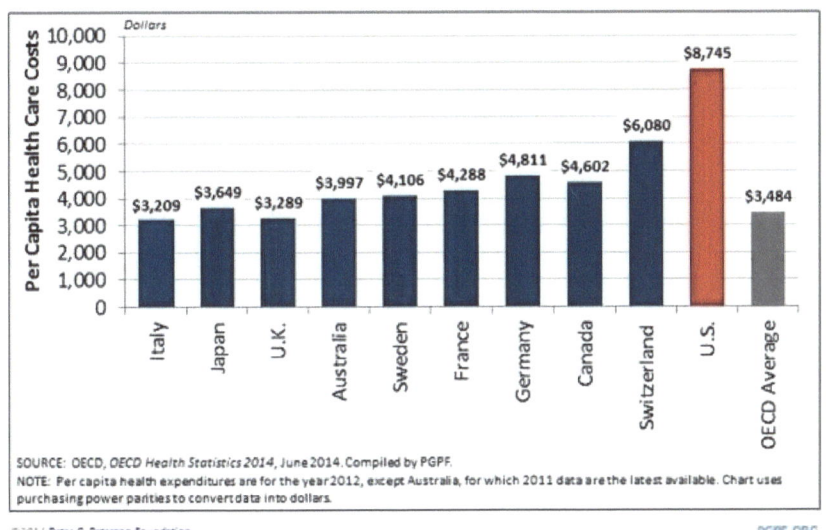

In fact, there currently about 143 million people, or 43 percent of the U.S. population, receiving single payer health insurance.

There are currently 74,600,261 individuals enrolled in Medicaid and CHIP in the U.S. as of March 2017. 68,965,776 individuals were enrolled in Medicaid and 5,634,485 individuals were enrolled in. Nearly 16.8 million additional individuals were enrolled in Medicaid and CHIP in March 2017 as compared to the period prior to the start of the first Marketplace open enrollment period (July - Sept. 2013), in the 49 states that reported relevant data for both periods, representing almost 30 percent increase over the baseline period (Medicade.gov).

Additionally, on its 50th anniversary, there were more than 55 million Americans covered by Medicare (7/28/2015 Centers for Medicare & Medicaid Services - www.cms.gov). This is up from 44 Million in 2007 (AARP)

Plus, the total number of VA medical enrollees as of 2014 was 9,111,955 (FAS.org, Congressional Research Service)

I am venturing a guess that the number of ACA enrollees who are below 200% poverty level and are receiving close to 100% premium and out of pocket reimbursement amounts to roughly 4 million people (kff.org).

Approximately 143 million people therefore currently have single payer health coverage - 43%! These are the same people who vocally threaten to throw out any politician who threatens to touch their benefits. These are the same people who are protesting in the streets in support of maintaining these benefits and entitlements.

Medicaid and CHIP Total Enrollment Chart - March 2017

The chart below displays the total number of individuals enrolled in Medicaid and the Children's Health Insurance Program (CHIP) in the current month and the period prior to the start of first Marketplace open enrollment period or "baseline" period (July – Sept. 2013). The total number of states that reported data for each period is also included. The enrollment figures are point-in-time counts (as of the last day of the month) and include only enrollees who received comprehensive benefit packages.

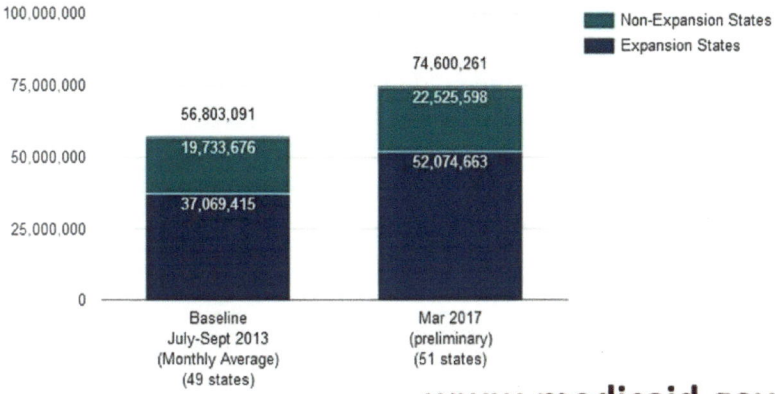

www.medicaid.gov

Stretching the Net

Percentage of U.S. population living in a household receiving some government benefit

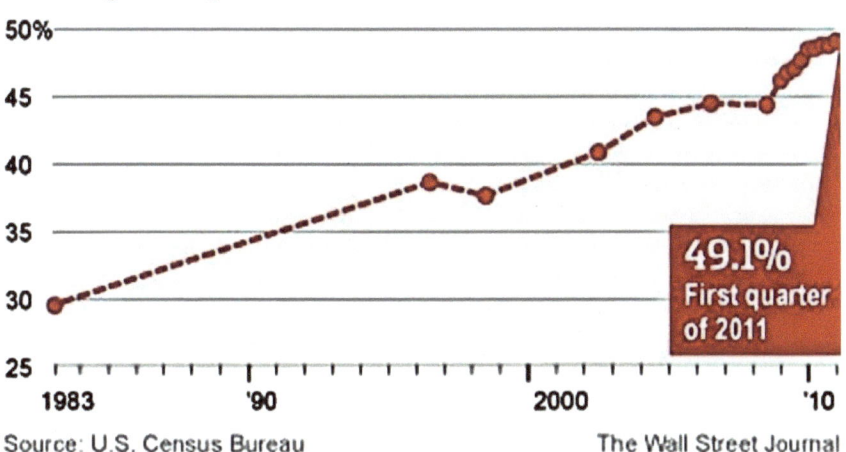

49.1%
First quarter of 2011

Source: U.S. Census Bureau   The Wall Street Journal

Benefits of Universal Healthcare

1. Smaller insurance infrastructure resulting in major reduction in the cost of the supporting infrastructure.
2. Shuttering of the entire infrastructure supporting the numerous federal, state and local healthcare insurance bureaucracies. All would be run by a single agency.
3. Universal coverage with no citizen denied healthcare when needed.
4. Guaranteed revenue stream for hospitals. No lost revenue due to inability of patients to pay.
5. A healthier country – reduced cost to business for lost days and reduced cost in critical emergency care services.
6. Fewer lives lost due to patients not getting required medical attention, accompanied by lower public assistance payments to families broken by illness and death.
7. Lower cost to business as no medical insurance would need to be provided. A small increase in business taxes could be implemented to help offset the cost of insurance. Also, reduced human resource cost as healthcare maintenance would be eliminated.
8. Lower cost to the elderly since there would be no Medicare out of pocket or need to purchase supplemental health insurance. Long term care would also be covered.

NOT FOR PROFIT!

In addition to removing the "middleman" from healthcare, we need to return to the not for profit format for hospitals. A hospital should be a community service, no less than the fire department or police force. Healthcare is a necessity for every person and should be universally available. No one should fear going to a doctor or hospital when they are sick, nor face bankruptcy if they do go to a hospital.

Some say the free market system can work if people are actually buying the insurance. This may be true, but in the end, the greed of the "for profit" corporations will in all probability rear its ugly head.

Neither option will work if not enough people are paying into the system, and taxpayer funded insurance policies don't count toward that goal.

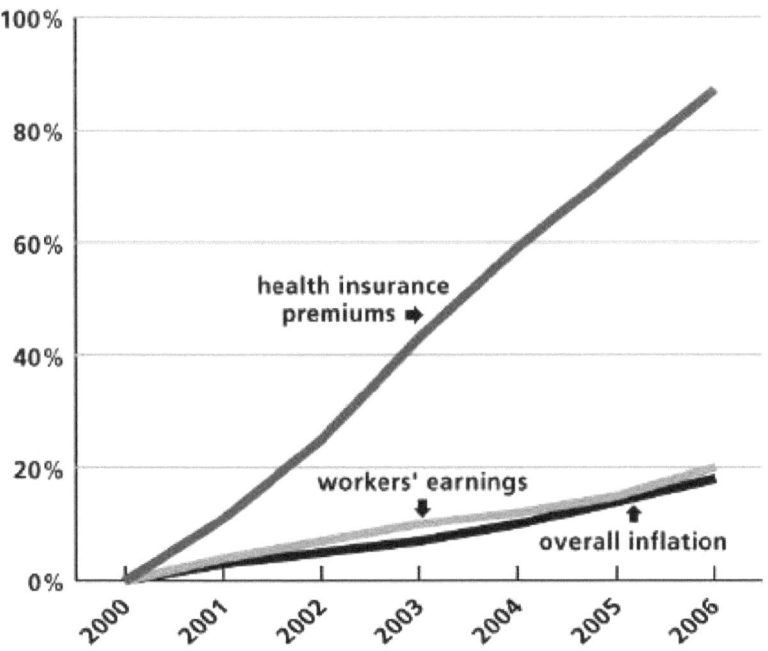

Figure 2

Medicare Benefit Payments, 2014

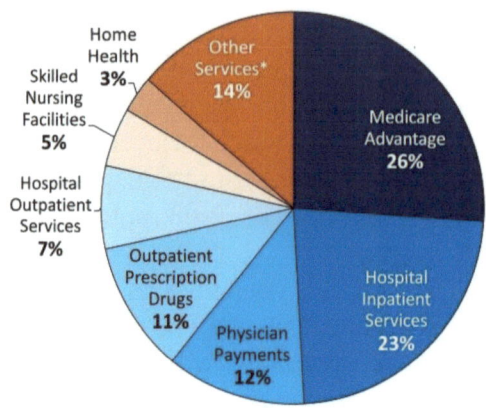

Total Medicare Benefit Payments, 2014 = $597 billion

NOTE: *Consists of Medicare benefit spending on hospice, durable medical equipment, Part B drugs, outpatient dialysis, ambulance, lab services, and other Part B services; also includes the effect of sequestration on spending for Medicare benefits and amounts paid to providers and recovered.
SOURCE: Congressional Budget Office, 2015 Medicare Baseline (March 2015).

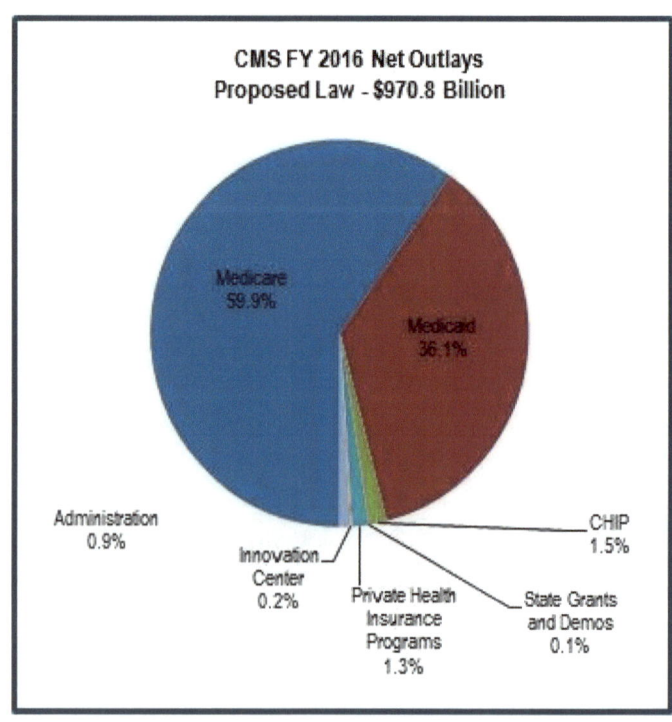

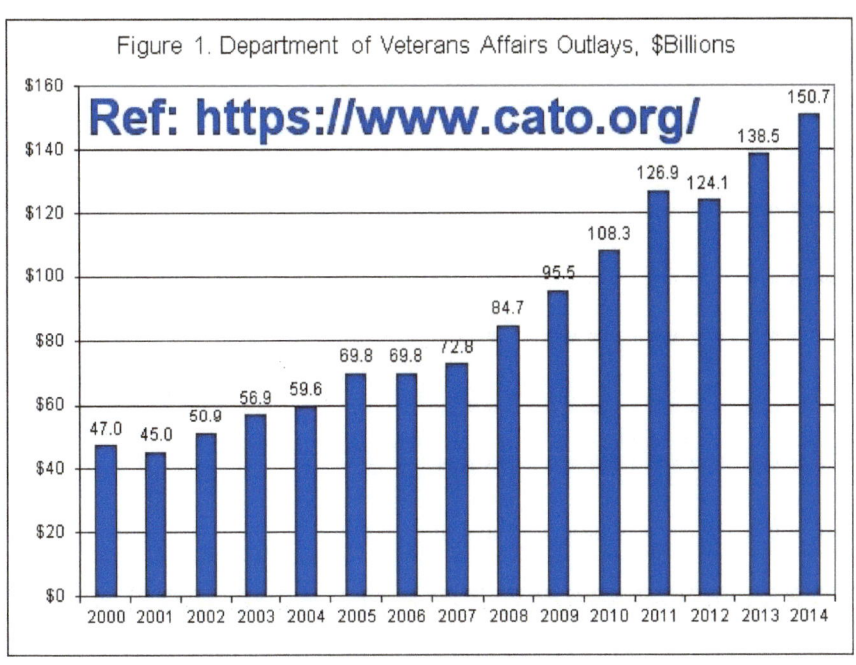

Figure 1. Department of Veterans Affairs Outlays, $Billions

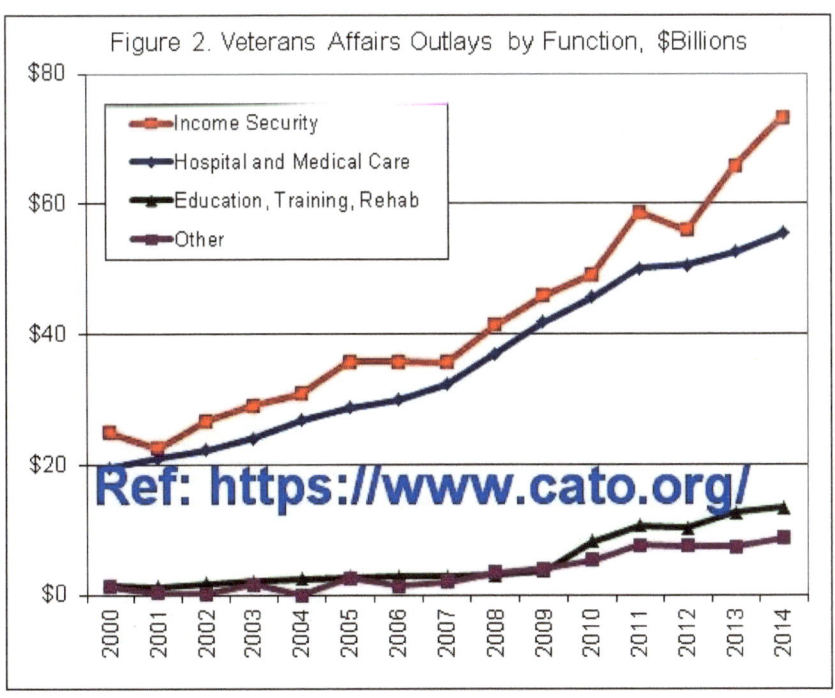

Figure 2. Veterans Affairs Outlays by Function, $Billions

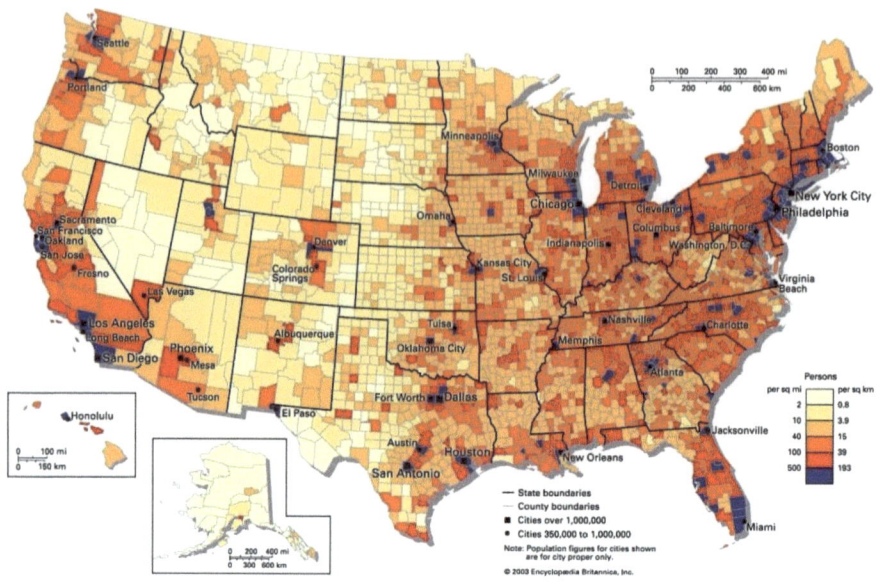

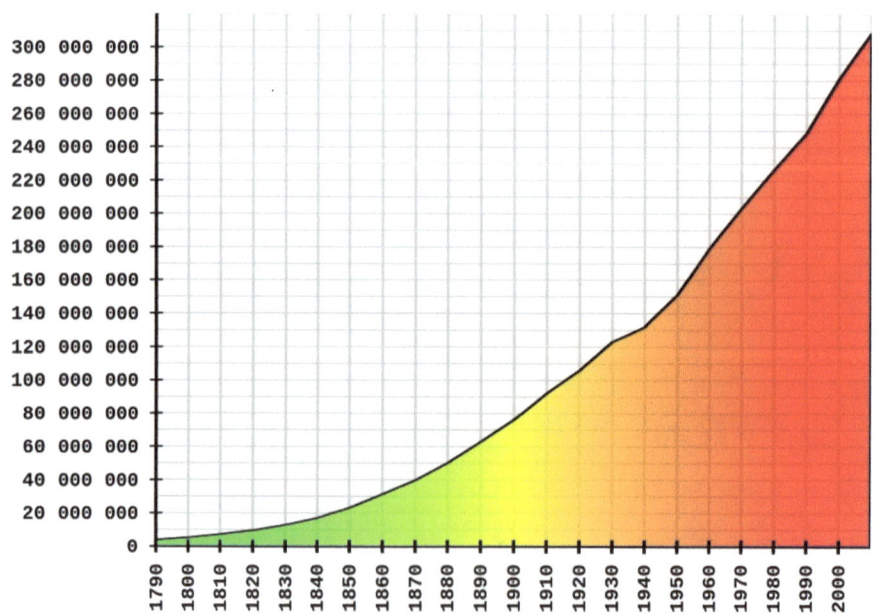

Chapter Nine

Postscript

Welfare state in the United Kingdom

From Wikipedia, the free encyclopedia

The **welfare state of the United Kingdom** comprises expenditures by the government of the United Kingdom intended to improve health, education, employment and social security. The British system has been classified as a liberal welfare state system.

> **The welfare state in the modern sense was anticipated by the Royal Commission into the Operation of the Poor Laws 1832 which found that the old poor law (a part of the English Poor laws) was subject to widespread abuse and promoted squalor, idleness and criminality in its recipients, compared to those who received private charity.** Accordingly, the qualifications for receiving aid were tightened up, forcing many recipients to either turn to private charity or accept employment.
>
> Opinions began to be changed late in the century by reports drawn up by men such as Seebohm Rowntree and Charles Booth into the levels of poverty in Britain. These reports indicated that in the massive industrial cities, between one-quarter and one-third of the population were living below the poverty line.

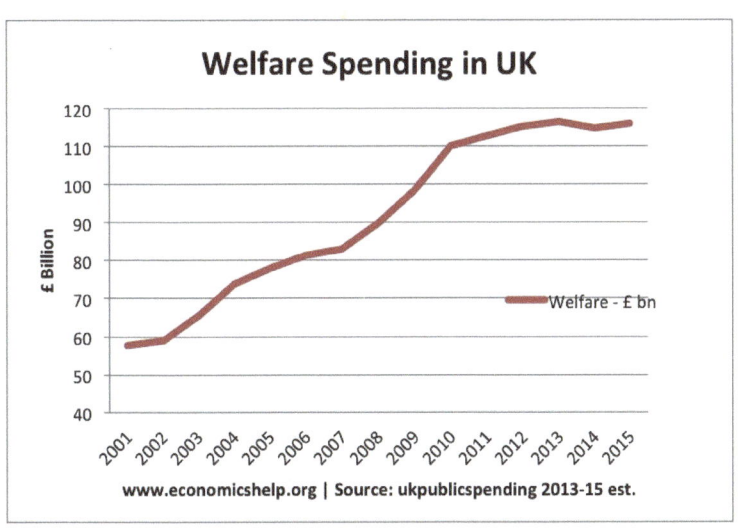

The smoking gun

The proof that if you want universal healthcare or affordable free market healthcare (or other tax funded benefits) you need to GO TO WORK and pay taxes! Without tax money there can be no taxpayer funded subsidies.

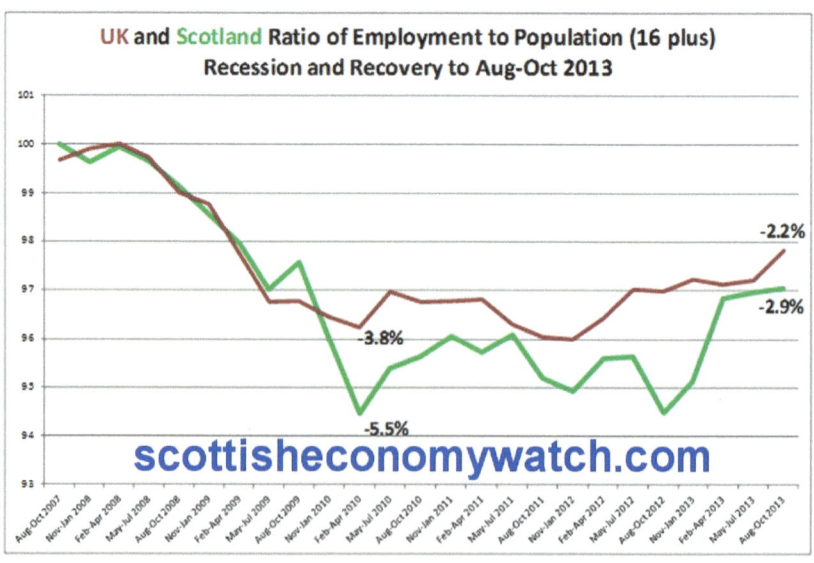

How does the UK percentage of employed citizens compare to the U.S.?

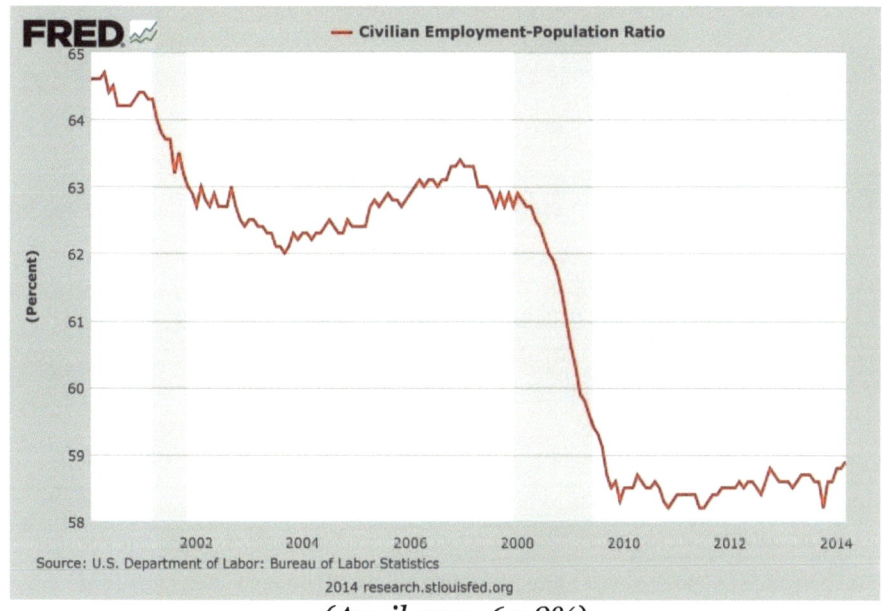

(April 2017 62.8%)

Take away:

There is no free lunch.

If you want something – you need to pay for it. To pay for it, you need to be employed.

Chapter Ten
Carl Marx

How do you tell a communist? Well, it's someone who reads Marx and Lenin. And how do you tell an anti-Communist? It's someone who understands Marx and Lenin.

Ronald Reagan 1987

****

Carl Marx, *Manifesto of the Communist Party* 1888

(Terms translated to modern English for clarity)

Modern capitalist society with its relations of production, of exchange and of property, a society that has conjured up such gigantic means of production and of exchange, is like the sorcerer, who is no longer able to control the powers of the nether world whom he has called up by his spells.

And how does the capitalist get over these crises? On the one hand enforced destruction of a mass of productive forces; on the other, by the conquest of new markets, and by the more thorough exploitation of the old ones. That is to say, by paving the way for more extensive and more destructive crises, and by diminishing the means whereby crises are prevented.

The weapons with which the capitalist felled feudalism to the ground are now turned against the capitalist itself.

But not only has the capitalist forged the weapons that bring death to itself; it has also called into existence the men who are to wield those weapons—the modern working class—the workers.

In proportion as the capitalist, i.e., capital, is developed, in the same proportion is the working class, the modern working class, developed—a class of laborers, who live only so long as they find work, and who find work only so long as their labor increases capital. These laborers, who must sell themselves piece-meal, are a commodity, like every other article of commerce, and are consequently exposed to all the vicissitudes of competition, to all the fluctuations of the market.

Owing to the extensive use of machinery and to division of labor, the work of the workers has lost all individual character, and consequently, all charm for the workman. He becomes an appendage of the machine, and it is only the most simple, most monotonous, and most easily acquired knack, that is required of him. Hence, the cost of production of a workman is restricted, almost entirely, to the means of subsistence that he requires for his maintenance, and for the propagation of his race. **But the price of a commodity, and therefore also of labor, is equal to its cost of production. In proportion therefore, as the repulsiveness of the work increases, the wage decreases.** Nay more, in proportion as the use of machinery and division of labor increases, in the same proportion the burden of toil also increases, whether by prolongation of the working hours, by increase of the work exacted in a given time or by increased speed of the machinery, etc.

Modern industry has converted the little workshop of the patriarchal master into the great factory of the industrial capitalist. Masses of laborers, crowded into the factory, are organized like soldiers. As privates of the industrial army they are placed under the command of a perfect hierarchy of officers and sergeants. Not only are they slaves of the capitalist class, and of the capitalist State; they are daily and hourly enslaved by the machine, by the over-looker, and, above all, by the individual capitalist manufacturer himself. The more openly this despotism proclaims gain to be its end and aim, the more petty, the more hateful and the more embittering it is.

The less the skill and exertion of strength implied in manual labor, in other words, the more modern industry becomes developed, the more is the labor of men superseded by that of women. Differences of age and sex have no longer any distinctive social validity for the working class. All are instruments of labor, more or less expensive to use, according to their age and sex.

No sooner is the exploitation of the laborer by the manufacturer, so far at an end, that he receives his wages in cash, than he is set upon by the other portions of the capitalist, the landlord, the shopkeeper, the pawnbroker, etc.

The lower strata of the middle class—the small tradespeople, shopkeepers, retired tradesmen generally, the handicraftsmen and peasants—all these sink gradually into the working class, partly because their diminutive capital does not suffice for the scale on which Modern Industry is carried on, and is swamped in the competition with the large capitalists, partly because their specialized skill is rendered worthless by the new methods of production. Thus the working class is recruited from all classes of the population.

The working class goes through various stages of development. With its birth begins its struggle with the capitalist. At first the contest is carried on by individual laborers, then by the workpeople of a factory, then by the operatives of one trade, in one locality, against the individual capitalist who directly exploits them. They direct their attacks not against the capitalist conditions of production, but against the instruments of production themselves; they destroy imported wares that compete with their labor, they smash to pieces machinery, they set factories ablaze, they seek to restore by force the vanished status of the workman of the Middle Ages.

The average price of wage-labor is the minimum wage, i.e., that quantum of the means of subsistence, which is absolutely requisite in bare existence as a laborer. What, therefore, the wage-laborer appropriates by means of his labor merely suffices to prolong and reproduce a bare existence. We by no means intend to abolish this personal appropriation of the products of labor, an appropriation that is made for the maintenance and reproduction of human life, and that leaves no surplus wherewith to command the labor of others. All that we want to do away with, is the miserable character of this appropriation, under which the laborer lives merely to increase capital, and is allowed to live only in so far as the interest of the ruling class requires it.

The development of Modern Industry, therefore, cuts from under its feet the very foundation on which the capitalist produces and appropriates products. **What the capitalist, therefore, produces, above all, is its own grave-diggers.** Its fall and the victory of the working class are equally inevitable.

Chapter Eleven
The Deep State

The Deep State, as defined by the writers who actually created the term, is the post-World War II entity consisting of Wall Street and London's banks and law firms, the state intelligence agencies they created and staffed, controlled corporate media, foundations, and think-tanks—a structure which intersects organized crime and certain sponsored politicians. It produces "deep" and universally destabilizing events in society, such as the assassination of John F. Kennedy, from which it apparently emerges unscathed.

Since Franklin Roosevelt's death, this entity's credo has been neoliberalism, a nihilistic, godless "philosophy" which promotes existentialism, pessimism, and a form of "freedom" which amounts to nothing more than personal narcissism, whether it be in the form of Ayn Rand's "egotism" or the self-realization mantras of the professional class. Having killed God, the random "free market" is alleged to reign over and determine the affairs of human beings. It seeks open borders (so that human labor can be had at the lowest possible wage) and free trade (so that goods might be produced at the cheapest price without regard to developing the economy or labor). That philosophy is otherwise embodied in Barack Obama's imperial dictum: "We set the rules," and in the failed economic nostrums of Friedrich von Hayek, Ludwig von Mises, and Milton Friedman.

(March 31, 2017 EIR *The Ideas Which Are Changing History*)

The lead feature article in the London Spectator on Jan. 21, 2017, the day after President Trump's inauguration.

References:

U.S. Department of Labor / Bureau of Labor and Industry

U.S. Bureau of Labor Statistics

U.S. Department of Health and Human Services

U.S. Department of Commerce

U.S. Census Bureau

March 31, 2017 EIR The Ideas Which Are Changing History

www.scottisheconomywatch.com

Heritage.org

Little Black Book of Billionaire Secrets

https://ivn.us/2012/02/16/an-aging-population-demographic-changes-in-america/

http://www.pewsocialtrends.org/2008/02/11/us-population-projections-2005-2050/

http://www.aoa.gov/aoaroot/aging_statistics/index.aspx

http://www.pewsocialtrends.org/2008/02/11/us-population-projections-2005-2050/

https://www.cia.gov/library/publications/the-world-factbook/geos/us.html

http://www.census.gov/population/www/pop-profile/natproj.html

https://www.forbes.com/sites/danielmitchell/2012/04/15/the-laffer-curve-shows-that-tax-increases-are-a-very-bad-idea-even-if-they-generate-more-tax-revenue/#646ca317e1c9

http://danieljmitchell.wordpress.com/2011/03/03/a-laffer-curve-tutorial/

http://danieljmitchell.wordpress.com/2010/06/29/we-all-know-government-is-too-big-but-heres-the-evidence/

https://www.forbes.com/sites/timworstall/2013/09/18/phew-the-robots-are-only-going-to-take-45-percent-of-all-the-jobs/#2478862356b1

http://www.technologyreview.com/view/519241/report-suggests-nearly-half-of-us-jobs-are-vulnerable-to-computerization/

http://www.rottentomatoes.com/m/american_jobs

https://en.wikipedia.org/wiki/Welfare_state_in_the_United_Kingdom

http://www.bls.gov/opub/ee/empearn201101.pdf

http://www.bls.gov/opub/mlr/2009/11/art3full.pdf.

https://www.dol.gov/wb/factsheets/qf-laborforce-10.htm

"Population Clock". United States Census Bureau. Retrieved January 23, 2017.

"United Nations - Population Division". un.org.

"Mean Center of Population for the United States: 1790 to 2000" (PDF). U.S. Census Bureau. Archived from the original (PDF) on 2001-11-03.

National Vital Statistics Reports. Births: Preliminary Data for 2015

"Median age of the U.S. population 1960-2015 - Statistic". statista.com.

"The White Population: 2000" (PDF). United States Census Bureau. August 2001.

"Statistical Abstract of the United States" (PDF). United States Census Bureau.
"U.S. population hits 300 million mark". MSNBC. Associated Press. 2006-10-17.

Morello, Carol and Mellnik, Ted. "Census: Minority Babies Are Now Majority in United States." Washington Post. May 17, 2012.

"Projected Population by Single Year of Age, Sex, Race, and Hispanic Origin for the United States: July 1, 2000 to July 1, 2050". U.S. Census Bureau.

"Not Just Black and White: Historical and Contemporary Perspectives on Immigration, Race, and Ethnicity in the United States". Nancy Foner, George M. Fredrickson (2005). p.120. ISBN 0-87154-270-6

"Immigrants in the United States and the Current Economic Crisis", Demetrios G. Papademetriou and Aaron Terrazas, Migration Policy Institute, April 2009.

"Immigration Worldwide: Policies, Practices, and Trends". Uma A. Segal, Doreen Elliott, Nazneen S. Mayadas (2010). Oxford University Press US. p. 32. ISBN 0-19-538813-5

Borjas, George J (2003). "Welfare reform, labor supply, and health insurance in the immigrant population". Journal of Health Economics. 22 (6): 933–958. doi:10.1016/j.jhealeco.2003.05.002. ISSN 0167-6296.

"CBO: 748,000 Foreign Nationals Granted U.S. Permanent Residency Status in 2009 Because They Had Immediate Family Legally Living in America Archived January 14, 2011, at the Wayback Machine.". CNSnews.com. January 11, 2011

""The First Measured Century: An Illustrated Guide to Trends in America, 1900–2000"". Public Broadcasting Service (PBS)

"Changing Face of Western Cities". The Washington Post. August 21, 2006.

"Non-white births outnumber white births for the first time in US". The Daily Telegraph. May 17, 2012

"American FactFinder Help: Hispanic or Latino origin". U.S. Census Bureau

"CIA - The World Factbook -- United States". CIA

"Recession may have pushed U.S. birth rate to a new low". USA Today. Associated Press

Births, Marriages, Divorces, and Deaths: Provisional Data for 2009 National Vital Statistics Reports Volume 58, Number 25

"Birthrate Is Lowest in a Century" Associated Press article printed in The New York Times August 27, 2010

Current Unemployment Rates for States and Historical Highs/Lows, U.S. Bureau of Labor Statistics

"Employment Situation Summary". U.S. Dept. of Labor. February 7, 2015

"Table A-15. Alternative measures of labor underutilization". U.S. Bureau of Labor.

https://data.bls.gov/timeseries/LNS11300000

https://www.usnews.com/news/the-report/articles/2015/07/16/unemployment-is-low-but-more-workers-are-leaving-the-workforce

https://www.marketplace.org/2012/10/11/economy/visual-history-us-workforce-1970-2012

https://www.cato.org/

www.ingramcontent.com/pod-product-compliance
Lightning Source LLC
Chambersburg PA
CBHW040322010626
45792CB00024B/2098